MANAGING WITHOUT MANAGERS

Volume 147, Sage Library of Social Research

RECENT VOLUMES IN
SAGE LIBRARY OF SOCIAL RESEARCH

106 Sanders **Rape & Women's Identity**
107 Watkins **The Practice of Urban Economics**
108 Clubb/Flanigan/Zingale **Partisan Realignment**
109 Gittell **Limits to Citizen Participation**
110 Finsterbusch **Understanding Social Impacts**
111 Scanzoni/Szinovacz **Family Decision-Making**
112 Lidz/Walker **Heroin, Deviance and Morality**
113 Shupe/Bromley **The New Vigilantes**
114 Monahan **Predicting Violent Behavior**
115 Britan **Bureaucracy and Innovation**
116 Massarik/Kaback **Genetic Disease Control**
117 Levi **The Coming End of War**
118 Beardsley **Conflicting Ideologies in Political Economy**
119 LaRossa/LaRossa **Transition to Parenthood**
120 Alexandroff **The Logic of Diplomacy**
121 Tittle **Careers and Family**
122 Reardon **Persuasion**
123 Hindelang/Hirschi/Weis **Measuring Delinquency**
124 Skogan/Maxfield **Coping With Crime**
125 Weiner **Cultural Marxism and Political Sociology**
126 McPhail **Electronic Colonialism**
127 Holmes **The Policy Process in Communist States**
128 Froland/Pancoast/Chapman/Kimboko **Helping Networks and Human Services**
129 Pagelow **Woman-Battering**
130 Levine/Rubin/Wolohojian **The Politics of Retrenchment**
131 Saxe/Fine **Social Experiments**
132 Phillips/Votey **The Economics of Crime Control**
133 Zelnik/Kantner/Ford **Sex and Pregnancy in Adolescence**
134 Rist **Earning and Learning**
135 House **The Art of Public Policy Analysis**
136 Turk **Political Criminality**
137 Macarov **Worker Productivity**
138 Mizruchi **The American Corporate Network**
139 Druckman/Rozelle/Baxter **Nonverbal Communication**
140 Sommerville **The Rise and Fall of Childhood**
141 Quinney **Social Existence**
142 Toch/Grant **Reforming Human Services**
143 Scanzoni **Shaping Tomorrow's Family**
144 Babad/Birnbaum/Benne **The Social Self**
145 Rondinelli **Secondary Cities in Developing Countries**
146 Rothman/Teresa/Kay/Morningstar **Marketing Human Service Innovations**
147 Martin **Managing Without Managers**
148 Schwendinger/Schwendinger **Rape and Inequality**
149 Snow **Creating Media Culture**
150 Frey **Survey Research by Telephone**

MANAGING WITHOUT MANAGERS

Alternative Work Arrangements in Public Organizations

Shan Martin

Volume 147
SAGE LIBRARY OF
SOCIAL RESEARCH

SAGE PUBLICATIONS
Beverly Hills / London / New Delhi

Copyright © 1983 by Sage Publications, Inc.

All rights reserved. No part of this book may be reproduced or utilized in any form or by any means, electronic or mechanical, including photo-copying, recording, or by any information storage and retrieval system, without permission in writing from the publisher.

For information address:

                      SAGE Publications, Inc.
                      275 South Beverly Drive
                      Beverly Hills, California 90212

SAGE Publications India Pvt. Ltd.   SAGE Publications Ltd
      C-236 Defence Colony   28 Banner Street
      New Delhi 110 024, India   London EC1Y 8QE, England

Printed in the United States of America

Library of Congress Cataloging in Publication Data

Martin, Shan.
   Managing without managers.

   (Sage library of social research ; v. 147)
   Bibliography: p.
   1. Management.   2. Public administration.
   3. Authority.   4. Employees' representation in
management.   I. Title.   II. Series.
HD38.M33185   1982   658   82-24017
ISBN 0-8039-1960-3
ISBN 0-8039-1961-1 (pbk.)

FIRST PRINTING

CONTENTS

Preface 7
Introduction 9
  1. The Aggrandizement of Management 17
  2. The Maintenance and Development Functions of Managers 33
  3. The Managing/Doing Dichotomy 43
  4. Perceptions of Supervision 61
  5. Cooperation Under the "Law of the Situation" 71
  6. The Erosion of Managerial Discretion 81
  7. Autonomous Work Groups 97
  8. Work Experiments in Private and Public Organizations 111
  9. The Myth of Management 125
10. Counteracting the Myth 135
11. An Alternative Approach to Work and Relationships in Public Organizations 153
Conclusion 173
Appendix A: Survey of Public Managers (background notes) 177
Appendix B: Summary of Managers' Responses to Survey Items by Type of Agency 179
Appendix C: Summary of Nonmanager's Responses to Survey Items by Type of Agency 185
Appendix D: Effects of Changes in Supervision as Rated by Nonmanagers 189
References 190
Name Index 195
Subject Index 197
About the Author 200

To the memory of my parents, and to Alex

PREFACE

Curtailing the cost and growth of government in the United States seems destined to be an issue that will dominate the domestic policy agenda of the 1980s. The beliefs of President Reagan and his advisers are adding new force to the familiar conviction, held by individuals and groups of diverse political persuasions, that there are serious things "wrong" with the government bureaucracy. Some federal programs have been terminated, others cut, and many others face an uncertain future. State and local governments are reducing their workforces and curbing other expenditures, eliminating some programs and services, and searching anxiously for new sources of revenue. They have thus far reacted with mixed emotions to the New Federalism, which promises a shift in discretionary power back to the state governments. The popular slogan of the current administration, "Let's get government off the backs of the people," continues to strike a responsive chord with most if not all citizens, and dramatic suggestions for doing just that are being aired and debated.

As shown in a report from the Office of Personnel Management in June 1980, government payroll and workforce figures are impressively large: The federal civilian payroll in the executive branch was estimated at $41 billion annually with approximately 2.9 million employees, excluding military personnel and the judicial and legislative branches (p. 2); state and local government payrolls were estimated at approximately $145 billion annually with almost 13 million employees (p. 15).

There have been small reductions in the total workforce at the federal level (McCurdy, 1982), a decline in the numbers of state and local government employees (Treadwell, 1981), and a decline in the annual growth rate of state and local government ("ACIR Identifies Public Sector Slowdown," 1982). Even if this trend continues, however, the government workforce is sufficiently large to be an important issue for some time to come.

The proposal for a reduction in the numbers and functions of public supervisors and managers contained in this book is not intended to support the popular movement to get government "off our backs." For the author, arguments in favor of eliminating excessive "layers" of management coexist quite comfortably with a belief that the service potential of government should not be cut as long as a need exists; in fact, we require better rather than fewer services for our citizens, and this is a goal that will surely require concerted effort on the part of both public and private interests.

If there is a rallying call underlying the material to be presented, it is to rid public agencies of unnecessary supervision, thus allowing the opportunity for government employees to function more successfully and more creatively at less cost to the taxpayers.

INTRODUCTION

This book is addressed to managers and nonmanagers, to those who supervise and to those who are supervised. It is also addressed to the men and women who study, teach, train, or consult with people in organizations. In fact, it is written for all those who are willing to reevaluate some of the common assumptions that underlie the hierarchy of authority and to consider some of the costs and quality of working-life consequences of that hierarchy.

My own interest in the supervisor- or manager-to-subordinate relationship grew out of a number of experiences occurring over a twelve-year period of working in and around organizations, and of interacting with students, many of whom were managers in large public agencies. One general characteristic of my experience during this time (beginning about 1970) was the extent to which those of us interested in the field of organization and management (either public or private) concentrated our attention on managers, particularly top managers. For most professors, students, consultants, researchers, and organization watchers interested in change or reform, this focus on managers continues, and understandably so. Apart from the good feelings derived from association with what are generally perceived to be "centers of power," there is a very practical consideration: Managers can provide access to organizations that might otherwise be unobtainable.

This focus on top managers has not precluded attention to other levels in the organization; there are many training programs for middle managers and for first-line supervisors. Less frequently (and usually at much greater expense), public organizations select more comprehensive approaches to change (such as organization development), which permit the study and modification of all aspects of the organization and at all levels. However, under most conditions, training or development efforts of any kind cannot be started (or funded) without the assistance or permission of top management. The literature on organizational development and other interventions associated with management training are replete with admonitions to the change agent to "begin at the top" by obtaining the support and, if possible, the active participation of top management.

This wise advice is not always easy to follow; those inexperienced with the process are usually surprised to discover that many (though by no means all) top managers who initiate a contact with a consultant, trainer, or educator, may very likely identify needs associated with levels other than their own. Later, when those lower in the organization are contacted, they will very likely point to management as needing improvement or as the obstacle to change. Although some top managers may politely excuse themselves from the analysis and improvement process, their importance is not diminished; change agents are left with a continuing need for their support in implementing any program, and more often than not, the consultant or educator (or an employee assigned to the project) will continue to pursue management involvement in order to ensure that the interventions selected will provide durable and significant improvements.

One problem with this preoccupation with approval and involvement from the top, and with the ability of managers to arrange various improvement programs for others but to avoid scrutiny of their own roles and functions, is that it tends to distract attention from an important question: Is it possible that we have too many managers and supervisors performing functions that are costly and unnecessary to the achievement of organizational objectives? In most of the literature on management (and in my own personal experience in consulting with organizations and teaching or training managers), it is not uncommon to make negative judgments about the competence of specific individuals within the management group or about particular methods of managing or supervising, but the *importance* of supervision and management in general is rarely questioned.

Persuading persons occupying management positions to include more subordinates in various decision processes remains a satisfactory goal for many consultants and educators who are convinced of the importance of management, but who are also convinced of the effectiveness of various forms of participative management. Concepts such as quality circles are based on the belief that workers have sound and creative ideas, and that a process should be established that would allow them to collaborate with managers in making decisions; increasingly, workers are encouraged to discuss, experiment, and present to management the substance of their suggestions. While I have always liked these approaches, my experiences in organizations have been leading me in another direction.

A turning point of sorts occurred one warm afternoon in the city yard of a medium-sized municipality in Southern California. (The yard contained offices and facilities for municipal utilities, maintenance and operations, and field maintenance personnel.) A colleague and I were conducting a citywide organizational assessment, and we were, on this afternoon, engaged in a group interview with maintenance workers, equipment operators, water production operators, meter readers, pump operators, tree trimmers, mechanics, and traffic painters. Many of those in attendance were angry and complained loudly about those who supervised them and about those above the supervisors who were managers.

The most memorable and most repeated sentiment expressed that day was: "We have no respect for our supervisors; they don't know what we are doing, and they don't know how to do anything *real*. They are yes-men to their managers, who do nothing but go to meetings and write reports." After giving numerous specific examples to illustrate these statements, the group's anger appeared to subside somewhat. One of the workers remarked that supervisors in his department invented work for themselves, as well as for those who report to them, in order to justify their coming to work every day and getting a paycheck. Some of the "made up" work included daily meetings to assign work, unnecessary reports and documentation, and making a "big deal" out of largely imagined disciplinary problems. This worker reminded me and my colleague that he and others in the room performed the *essential* functions of each of the three departments represented, and that they knew from experience and observation more of what needed to be done each day than did any of the supervisors. Also, they knew *how* to do it.

There are many ways of "explaining" the sentiments expressed that afternoon. Listening to antimanagement statements from groups of workers was certainly not a new experience for me, just as I was quite accustomed to hearing derogatory comments from managers and supervisors about workers. However, the frustration and bitterness accompanying the words were stronger than usual. I speculated initially that the disposition of the group had been unduly influenced by a few articulate malcontents. I was told later that a few of the men in the group interviewed did indeed have reputations as troublemakers, but this turned out to be just a small part of what was going on.

After contacting members of other departments and the city manager and his staff, I learned that the supervision and management of those interviewed was generally recognized throughout the organization as being extremely poor. At this point, I began to think more carefully about the substance of the workers' complaints and to wonder how many other organizations employ well-paid supervisors who "don't know how to do anything real," and even more highly paid managers who do not perform the important functions that the literature and popular belief proclaim.

As a result of this experience, I began to question the *need* for supervision in other organizations, to evaluate the functions of managers more carefully, and to analyze the hierarchy of authority. In subsequent contacts, informal observations, and surveys, I found that data from other organizations tended to support the basic message from the workers in the city yard: *We can perform our work without supervision.*

Another important factor that was pulling me away from consideration of the more traditional organizational reforms (and pushing me toward this study) was a growing awareness of the plight of government organizations in an era of decreasing resources and increasing disenchantment with the cost, size, and perceived wastefulness of public bureaucracies. Two major approaches have been utilized in reducing the size and cost of government. The first approach is to increase the productivity of government workers and the efficiency and effectiveness of programs and procedures, with the objective of reducing costs and improving performance. If successful, these measures are expected either to reduce the expenditures required for the same output, or to increase the output from the same expenditure. The outcome of a productivity effort may be to reduce the size of the workforce or (in better times) to redistribute resources in such a way that the "savings" accomplished in the successful program can be used subsequently to support additional programs, positions, or services.

A second approach, short of termination of an agency or department, is simply to reduce budget allocations in keeping with reduced revenue, which in many cases results in a smaller workforce and decreases in the frequency, quantity, or quality of public goods or services. Typically, service cutbacks are the stated consequences of a reduced workforce, necessitated in turn by budget cuts. An immediate reduction in the workforce is usually accomplished by layoffs at the lowest levels of the organization, while a gradual reduction is accomplished through attrition; vacancies due to resignations or retirements are not filled.

In many organizations, of course, public employees are called on to maintain or even increase their service output with fewer numbers of employees, less money, less space, and depleted or deteriorating equipment (that is, to do "more with less"). Frequently, the productivity approach, more moderate in nature and reflecting more abundant resources, is the precursor of the budget-cut approach, which is the more drastic and increasingly utilized action reflecting sharply diminishing resources and an increasingly negative attitude toward government on the part of some political leaders and the public.

In this book, an additional strategy will be explored, one in which the roles in the existing workforce can be reconceptualized in such a way that a minimally successful outcome would be lower salary costs (which would substantially reduce total organizational costs) without service cuts, and a fully successful outcome would be lower salary costs, improved quality of services to the public, and improved quality of working life for the government workforce. It differs from productivity measures and budget cuts in that these actions have been taken in public organizations largely without disturbing popular notions associated with the manager- or supervisor-to-subordinate relationship and the hierarchy of authority.

The strategy recommended in this study involves redistributing the managing functions and increasing the frequency of "doing" activities; this approach has, by and large, been overlooked as a potential source of reduction in the cost of government. In recent years, quality circles and various participation mechanisms often save money through suggestions made by teams of workers and supervisors organized for that purpose; these techniques have the added advantage of improving the morale of the workers, an improvement attributed in part to the fact that the process opens avenues of participation formerly closed. For many, the most important advantage of quality circles and other kinds of worker participation is that such programs do not require any modification of the formal hierarchical structure. (Consideration will be given in Chapter 11 to the question of whether or not the change in the informal structure brought about by the introduction of advisory worker groups can be considered a step toward the more radical structural changes of the kind recommended in this study.)

It should be apparent from these introductory comments that the approach recommended in this book goes beyond participation; it is my opinion that reducing the numbers and functions of managers and supervisors has the potential for cost savings over and above those realized by traditional productivity measures, and that both the cost-saving potential and improvements in the quality of working life will be more basic and more durable when utilizing self-management forms than when relying on participative management or advisory worker groups. Four assumptions underlie these claims: (1) In the long run, workers will not remain satisfied with merely "participating" with management at the latter's invitation, nor with giving advice to enhance productivity (or profits). (2) There are many benefits and challenges to be realized from various adaptations of self-management; these benefits and challenges remain virtually untapped in the public sector. (3) The salaries attached to unnecessary manager and supervisor positions represent a substantial and enduring savings once the positions are eliminated. (4) A great deal of time and energy now absorbed in management and supervision activities can be released through the elimination of unnecessary positions and the redistribution of necessary functions to workers; this will allow more individuals to give attention to what I believe to be the essential or "doing" functions of the organization.

The information, opinions, and suggestions contained in this book are all linked, one way or another, with the interview in the City Yard, and with the need to reduce the costs of government. The aggrandizement of management (Chapter 1) has created obstacles to rethinking the functions of managers, and some data are available to suggest that, contrary to the image generated in the literature, managers spend more time maintaining than developing organizations (Chapter 2). In Chapter 3, the separation of managing from doing, long considered a sacrosanct law of management, is explored; evidence is presented that suggests a disproportionate growth in the upper-middle levels of organizations (those who manage rather than do). The necessity of supervision is questioned, and the ambivalence expressed by some who receive supervision is explored: Many workers *want* to have a supervisor; they just do not *need* one (Chapter 4). The idea that cooperation in organizations works better than control is revived by exposure to the thinking of Mary Parker Follett and Chester Barnard (Chapter 5).

The erosion of managerial discretion, especially in making nonroutine decisions, is discussed from several different perspectives, including that of the manager who is prone to complain, "My hands are tied" (Chapter 6). Some information about work redesign that results in autonomous or semi-autonomous work groups is presented in Chapter 7, and examples of experiments in various forms of work redesign and worker participation in both public and private organizations are provided in Chapter 8. All of the propositions from the preceding chapters are reviewed in Chapter 9, which includes an elaboration of the myth of management. Arguments intended to convince the reader of the viability of a self-managing approach to work in public organizations are brought together in Chapter 10, and the final chapter is devoted primarily to describing how that approach might be implemented in real organizations.

Throughout the book, a general theme is that one of the things wrong with public organizations is the way in which they perpetuate an unnecessary hierarchy of authority. An assessment of the human and service costs inherent in the traditional superordinate/subordinate relationship will, it is hoped, create interest in changes more basic, and at the same time more circumscribed, than those usually found in the management or administrative reform literature. The dimensions of particular interest are in changing the imposed separation of managing from doing toward an integration of the two, and from a work environment dominated by control and dependency toward a work environment in which interactions are governed by goals, by the nature of the work, and by the talents and interests of the workers.

CHAPTER 1

THE AGGRANDIZEMENT OF MANAGEMENT

The emergence of management in this century may have been a pivotal event of history.

—Peter Drucker

The idea that managers are absolutely essential to organizations has been persuasively incorporated into almost every aspect of public and business administration. It has reached mythological proportions in the sense that it has become part of the ideology of our society. Before examining the gap between the myth and what managers themselves report as "reality," some examples will be offered of commonly held views of management that have dominated the literature, captured the popular imagination, and led to the aggrandizement of the role and functions of managers.

The views of management presented in this chapter will be referred to collectively as traditional, not because they are older or necessarily more conservative than others, but because they tend to dominate the field, and because they start with the premise that management functions and those who perform them are of supreme importance to organizations and to society. From that unquestioned premise, most of the writers in this group proceed to explain, analyze, and categorize the functions they believe managers perform. In relatively rare instances, they use empirical methods of finding out what managers do, typically not as a challenge to the importance of their activities, but as a means of providing more accurate explanations, analyses, or categories, and more relevant training and education for existing and aspiring managers.

For the purposes of this chapter, the word *manager* will be used as it is in much of the literature to mean a person in a public or private organization who directs, controls, plans, coordinates, or evaluates organizational activities. Our objective at this point is not to distinguish between top managers, middle managers, or supervisors (although that distinction is very important for some analyses), but rather to capture the spirit of what has been written about managers in order to discuss later how that spirit has shaped the nature of the superordinate/subordinate relationship at whatever level it is found in organizations.

> ***Proposition 1:*** The belief that managers are supremely important to organizations has dominated the literature.

Before attempting to divide the vast amount of material comprising the traditional view of management into subsections that will be useful for a better understanding of how these views have aggrandized the role of manager, a few of the typical comments that flood the literature are cited to convey the prevalent mood and sentiment.

> The scope of the world's and America's problems is such that they will only be solved through large organizations. Managers in large public and private business, governments, and nonprofit institutions will play the central role in mobilizing and directing the human and material resources that are necessary to cure the conditions about which so many are concerned, young and old alike [Webber, 1979, p. 8].
>
> Never in the whole history of the world has the art of management been as difficult as it is in these times.... There is no single more constructive course of action, no more complex pro-

fession, no more demanding responsibility than that of management [Salzmann, 1969, p. 20].

But no organization can function without a consolidation of power in the relationship of a central figure with his select group [Zalenznik, 1970/1973, p. 720].

Management is the specific organ of the modern institution . . . on the performance of which the performance and the survival of the institution depend [Drucker, 1974, p. 6].

No job is more vital to our society than that of the manager. It is the manager who determines whether our social institutions serve us well or whether they squander our talents and resources [Mintzberg, 1975, p. 61].

Within the climate set by these and similar comments, writers have analyzed and categorized what managers do. To the extent that reforms have been proposed, they have usually occurred within the context of the importance (necessity) of management. More germane to the theme of this study is the fact that a growing number of individuals within organizations have, for various reasons, been perceived and trained as managers with the effect that the importance originally linked with a select group at the top has spread downward. Thus an interest in changing the superordinate/subordinate relationship at any level must begin with an examination of how the role of manager, or of management, has been conceived. One way of doing that is to develop a composite profile from the literature of an ideal manager, and the three categories that best lend themselves to this task are: (1) the functions, behavior, and roles of managers; (2) the traits and skills of managers; and (3) the decisions of managers.

The Manager's Role: Traditional Descriptions

FUNCTIONS, BEHAVIOR, AND ROLES

Of all the general functions of managers, those of planning, organizing, directing, and controlling are the most enduring categories found in the literature. With some occasional modification, they continue to appear in every text, training course, and review on management. The father of this approach is said to be Henri Fayol, who in 1916 identified five functions: planning, organizing, coordinating, commanding, and controlling. In the 1930s, Luther Gulick (who celebrated his 90th birthday in January 1982) added to this list and came up with his famous POSDCORB: planning, organizing, staffing, directing, coordinating, reporting, and budgeting (Gulick, 1937).

It is interesting to note that from the POSDCORB list, the three functions that rarely show up in modern lists are staffing and reporting (subsumed under organizing), and budgeting (subsumed under controlling). These are more specific, "hands-on" or "doing" functions than are the others, and may have been deemed by later theorists (or managers) to be activities better left for those in lower-level positions. There are many warnings in both old and new books on management and in management training courses against doing.

There are, of course, variations in descriptions of the functions managers are expected to perform. Katz and Kahn used the term "coordination" in describing two of the three basic management functions: (1) coordination of substructures, (2) resolution of conflicts between hierarchical levels, and (3) cooordination of external requirements with organizational resources and needs (1966, p. 94).

Categories such as those used by Katz and Kahn are more representative of a body of literature on management that deals with organizations as social systems existing in a complex and always changing environment. In this newer literature, the province of management is typically expanded to include the external environment. Writers have moved away from an earlier preoccupation with variations of POSDCORB and with treating organizations as if they were closed systems. The emphasis has shifted to recognition of the permeable nature of the boundaries between organizations and their environments, and of the need for organizations to be proactive and innovative, to be able to create change as well as to adapt to it. This shift added new dimensions to the functions managers were expected to perform.

Another characteristic of the literature on organizations is the tendency to consider public and private management as being virtually indistinguishable as far as the principles of the discipline are concerned. Drucker points out that managers everywhere face the same kind of tasks, i.e., to give direction to the institution, to set its objectives, and to organize resources in order to produce the results for which the organization exists (1974, p. 17). This tendency is noticeable in the introductions to many recent books on management, organizations, or organizational behavior; public sector managers are included in the intended audience, and the books are likely to contain whole sections relating to public organizations. The settings for case studies and exercises in which a particular aspect of management is explored are usually both public and private; these may include manufacturing firms, educational institutions, government agencies, hospitals, banks, transportation firms, space laboratories, insurance companies, or the military.

Literature on the functions of managers has been supplemented by studies of leader or manager behavior, such as Ohio State University's long-term study of the behavior of leaders begun in 1946. Lists of descriptive statements about leaders were classified in the early stages under nine dimensions, with a total of 150 statements or items from which respondents could choose. These nine dimensions were later reduced to three: maintenance of membership, objective attainment, and group interaction facilitation. Eventually, after further studies, two dimensions were identified as being important in describing leader behavior (Shartle, 1956, pp. 115-120): initiating structure interaction (sometimes referred to as the goal attainment aspect of leadership) and consideration (sometimes referred to as human relations).

Leonard Sayles studied managerial work, classifying it into three major categories: Manager as a (1) participant in the external work flows, (2) leader or initiator who gives directions, responds, or intervenes, and (3) monitor (1964/1980, pp. 49-54). A more recent categorization by roles is offered by Mintzberg, who thought highly of the work done by Sayles. He identifies three groups of roles with subsets (1973: 75-79): (1) interpersonal (figurehead, liaison, and leader), (2) informational (monitor, disseminator, and spokesperson), and (3) decisional (entrepreneur, disturbance handler, resource allocator, and negotiator).

Generally speaking, finding out what managers actually do (how they spend their time) is a more recent and rarer phenomenon than describing their functions, behavior, or roles in broad categories. The search for evidence of what managers do is sometimes called the empirical school. Mintzberg and others have pointed out that two basic methods have been used: (1) asking managers to respond to (by questionnaires) or keep track of (by logs or diaries) some preestablished categories of activities, or (2) having the researcher observe a manager, an incident, or activities in organizations and determine a method of sorting out the observations before or after the data are collected. There are advantages and disadvantages to all methods, and while almost everyone would agree that specific information about the activities of managers is preferable to descriptions of what someone thinks they do or should do, carrying out research on the work performed by managers is not an easy task.

The diary method, utilized in the first noteworthy empirical study by Carlson in 1951, has been the most popular method. Of fourteen empirical studies of managerial work activity from 1951 to 1968, ten were some variant of the diary method, one was activity sampling, and three were by observation (Mintzberg, 1973, p. 23). The method chosen by Mintzberg in his intensive study of five chief executives was that of structured observation (1973, pp. 231-237). Some of the findings from his research were popularized in 1975 by the *Harvard Business Review,* and included the following: Managers are action oriented rather than reflective, they work at an unrelenting pace, their activities are characterized by variety, discontinuity, and brevity, they have little use for aggregated written information and prefer obtaining information in telephone calls and meetings, and their methods of decisions, processing information, and scheduling time are not systematic or scientific but "locked deep inside their brains" (p. 53).

Mintzberg appropriately points out the weaknesses inherent in the traditional approach of listing abstract words or categories to describe the functions of managers, one of which is that this method does not enlighten us about what managers actually do. In presenting his findings in 1975, he uses a format of "folklore" versus "fact," and makes a convincing argument about the necessity of obtaining evidence about specific activities rather than accepting generalizations. In spite of his critical stance with respect to some aspects of the traditional view, Mintzberg does not question the importance or necessity of what managers do; he demonstrates that they perform their functions differently (as well as perform different functions) than lists such as POSDCORB suggest.

The empirical studies about what managers do are quite modest in number compared with the vast numbers of books and articles about managers and management. Most, though not all, such studies have been conducted with business leaders or managers. Of the public sector studies, one involved 194 army civilians classified roughly as middle management (Katzell, Barrett, Vann, & Hogan, 1968). In the research, various role dimensions, such as planning, staffing, budgeting, time with others, and controlling, were examined in relationship to organizational variables such as mission, level, size, and stability. Results showed that "organizational features most prominently associated with variations in role included the mission and level of the organization, the job family of the executive, and his span of control. The role dimensions which were most prone to vary with the situation were staffing, controlling, and time spent with others" (p. 22).

Mintzberg's study (1973, pp. 230-277) included a school superintendent, and the categories he utilized formed the basis of at least two subsequent studies in which public sector organizations and personnel were involved. One was a study of 370 top civilian executives in the navy (Lau, Newman, & Broedling, 1980). Like their private sector counterparts, navy executives work at a very fast pace on a variety of fragmented activities, favor direct oral communication over other kinds, and "have insufficient time to devote to leadership activities, long-range planning, and/or the influence and definition of organizational policies and goals.... Much time is spent reacting to short-term crises, to demands imposed by superiors, and to what executives regard as unnecessary meetings, red tape, and bureaucratic trivia" (p. 519).

A second study was described in a paper presented to the Academy of Management (Kurke & Aldrich, 1979) and involved four chief executives in a public hospital, a school system, a high technology manufacturing firm, and a bank. Mintzberg's categorizations were used whenever feasible, and the results showed great similarity with this findings: Managers perform a great quantity of work with little free time, work is characterized by brevity, variety, and fragmentation, and managers favor verbal over written communication. One finding of special interest is that in Mintzberg's study, subordinates consume about one-third to one-half of a manager's time, and from one-third to three-quarters in the Aldrich and Kurke study. "These contacts involved requests, sending or receiving information, and occasionally strategy-making" (Kurke & Aldrich, 1979, p. 7). To some extent, this corroborates findings from a survey of public managers (Martin, 1981) in which contacts with subordinates was the most frequent activity out of eighteen possible activities in which those managers engaged. The profile of public managers that emerged from that survey will be described in more detail in the next chapter.

TRAITS AND SKILLS

In 1953, when interest in the traits of managers was high, Argyris interacted with numerous American executives and came up with a list of ten characteristics of successful executives. He found that they exhibit a high tolerance for frustration, encourage participation and do not threaten the personal worth of others, continually question themselves in order to learn from their failures as well as from their successes, understand and do not feel threatened by "competitive warfare," express hostility tactfully, control emotions over a victory, are not shattered by defeat, understand the necessity for limits and for unfavorable decisions, identify themselves with groups for a sense of security and stability, and set goals realistically (Argyris, 1953, pp. 50-54).

In 1958, *Fortune* carried an article in which executive qualities or traits were identified on the basis of a questionnaire survey of 150 high-ranking executives (Stryker, 1958). These executives considered the following fourteen traits indispensable: judgment, initiative, foresight, integrity, energy drive, human relations skill, decisiveness, dependability, objectivity, emotional stability, fairness, ambition, dedication, and cooperation (p. 189).

Lists of qualities or characteristics such as these were fairly common in the 1950s, but in recent years there have been very few enthusiastic supporters of the "superior traits" school. For one thing, the correlation of specific personality traits with managerial success has been tested, and no consistent correlation has been found. A generally accepted view is that, regardless of personal characteristics, managers' chances for success will be enhanced by periodic education or training in some specific or technical aspects of managerial work, or by an updated overview of the field of management. Typically, those who are instructing or consulting emphasize a number of contingency or situational factors, only one of which might be the individual manager's personal characteristics. (With this perspective in mind, the belief that managers must possess certain innate qualities was very likely doomed to early extinction, not only because of lack of evidence to support such a belief, but also because of its potential for diminishing the need for schools of management, for management training, and for the services of management consultants.)

This shift from innate traits to broad skills (much like the previously mentioned shift in emphasis from prescribed internal managerial functions to flexible, wide-ranging functions that include interactions with the environment) is part of the more recent portrayal of a manager as one who is enmeshed in a number of different and complex organizational relationships. The skills most likely to be needed by such a manager are: peer skills (maintaining peer relationships), leadership skills, conflict resolution skills, skills in decision making under ambiguity, resource allocation skills, entrepreneurial skills, information-processing skills, and skills of introspection (Mintzberg, 1973, pp. 189-193).

In some of the literature, skills sound much like functions: strategic planning, communication within the organization, and making decisions under conditions of uncertainty (Drucker, 1974, p. 17). Drucker contrasts skills with understanding by pointing out that a manager who has only the skills and techniques and does not understand the fundamentals of the discipline is not a manager.

Robert Katz (1955/1974) adds a different dimension by linking skill categories with administrative levels. There are three skills needed by an effective administrator: (1) technical skill, which involves specialized knowledge and the ability to work with processes or physical objects (p. 91); (2) human skills, which include the ability to build cooperative effort and to communicate with and understand the words and behavior of others (pp. 91-92); and (3) conceptual skill, which is the coordinating and integrating of all the activities and interests of the organization toward common objectives, recognizing the interdependence of various internal functions. Conceptual skill also involves visualizing the relationship of the organization to key elements in the external environment including the "political, social, and economic forces of the nation as a whole" (p. 93). All three are important, but "at lower levels of administrative responsibility, the principal need is for technical and human skills. At higher levels, technical skill becomes relatively less important while the need for conceptual skill increases rapidly. At the top level of an organization, conceptual skill becomes the most important skill of all for successful administration" (p. 96), whereas "human skill, the ability to work with others, is essential to effective administration at every level" (p. 95).

Making much the same point, and using the same three categories in relation to three levels of management—top, middle, and supervisor—Hersey and Blanchard (1977) point out that while "the amount of technical and conceptual skills needed at these different levels of management varies, *the common denominator that appears to be crucial at all levels is human skill*" (pp. 6-7). With regard to the other two skill categories, conceptual and technical, the authors conclude that the functions of top managers require more conceptual skill than is required by either of the other levels, while the supervisor requires significantly more technical and less conceptual skill than do either top or middle managers.

This division of skill requirements and the determination of their relative importance at the various levels is an essential part of the conventional wisdom of management. In ensuing chapters, the point will be made that public managers have negligible discretion in the use of their conceptual skills in influencing the goals and direction of their organization, and that the importance of human relations skills as they are commonly taught and practiced has been greatly exaggerated.

DECISIONS

Simon is undoubtedly the theorist who comes to mind when the focus of attention is on decision making in organizations. He views it as the key to the analysis and control of organizations by management. The important message is that if a manager controls the premises of the decisions of others in the organization, his or her management job is made much easier because of the reduced need for close supervision of subordinates. As Simon expresses it, "The organization trains and indoctrinates its members. This might be called the 'internalization' of influence, because it injects into the very nervous systems of the organization members the criteria of decision that the organization wishes to employ" (Simon, 1976, p. 103).

A familiar method of studying the decision-making functions of managers, used by Simon and many others, is to classify two broad types of organizational decisions as routine and nonroutine. Selznick moved in that direction 25 years ago by distinguishing between administrative management and institutional leadership:

> Efficiency as an operating ideal presumes that goals are settled and that the main resources and methods for achieving them are available. The problem is then one of joining available means to known ends. This order of decision-making we have called *routine,* distinguishing it from the realm of *critical* decision. The latter, because it involves choices that affect the basic character of the enterprise, is the true province of leadership as distinct from administrative management [Selznick, 1957, p. 135].

The fact that certain kinds of decisions seem to be routine and suitable for programming has led some managers to seek the advantages of a programmed approach, usually with the aid of a computer. As has been pointed out, this move is not without its price. "Routine or programmed approaches to decision making cannot provide optimal solutions, for they are bound to simplify and generalize a broad array of situations and events. However, they do result in a greater degree of coordination, protection, and reduction in cost for the overall organization" (Ivancevich, Szilagyi, & Wallace, 1977, p. 391).

If one has a traditional, supportive view of managers, the dramatic increase in the use of computers within organizations can be evaluated as having the potential advantage of releasing managers from routine decisions; as a consequence, they can give more attention to those decisions still surrounded by uncertainty that require their special skills, such as those in the areas of long-range planning, the conceptualization of current and anticipated problems, or human relations. The point will be made later that many public managers not only continue to make routine decisions (with and without the aid of computers), but they also lack (or do not use) the discretion to make many of the important nonroutine decisions suitable to their skills and salaries.

Terms made popular by Lindblom that reflect concern more with how managers and others make decisions than with categories of decisions are "muddling through" or "incrementalism" (1959, 1968). Lindblom's argument is that the only way to respond to uncertainty and complexity is incrementally. The inability (limited rationality as Simon would say) of mortal beings to solve the interrelated and changing problems facing organizations today limits us to decision making on a piecemeal (satisficing) basis. Lindblom sees the individual (and presumably manager) as a "shrewd, resourceful problem-solver who is wrestling bravely with a universe that he is wise enough to know is too big for him" (Lindblom, 1968, p. 27). Thus, whatever the existing decision-making limitations, they are attributable to the constantly changing and complex environment rather than to any correctable deficiency in managers.

In the same vein, but obviously geared more to the practitioner, another writer believes that "good managers don't make policy decisions" (Wrapp, 1967). He sees managers as opportunists who muddle through problems, but with a purpose. Unlike many writers, he portrays good managers as those who enmesh themselves in many operating matters and do not limit themselves to the big organizational picture. He concludes that good managers, in moving toward organizational goals, keep open many pipelines of information, concentrate on a limited number of significant issues, identify corridors of comparative indifference (which will permit them action with less risk), give the organization a sense of direction with openended objectives, and spot opportunities in the midst of operating problems and decisions (p. 98). His basic warning is: "If he [the manager] follows the advice to free himself from operations, he may soon find himself subsisting on a diet of abstractions leaving the choice of what he eats in the hands of his subordinates" (p. 92). These descriptions of the kinds of activities good managers should engage in as well as avoid appear to be a rare obfuscation of the managing-not-doing advice, and a reinforcement of Simon's advice that managers should give, not receive, the premises of decisions.

Summary

What conclusions can be drawn from this brief review of some of the traditional descriptions of managers found in the literature? Taken together, they create an image of a manager as the motor of the organizational machine, or the heart, brain, and other vital organs of the organizational body, whose job it is to keep all the other parts "going." Top managers perform certain duties, but they also serve as symbols of organizational unity and purpose. The characteristics attributed to (or discovered in) managers are diligence, decisiveness, self-confidence, humaneness, intelligence, toughness, and the ability to introspect.

"Management" is inextricable from "organization"; organizations are necessary to society in carrying out its objectives, and, therefore, managers are important to society. The functions of managers as defined by theory and research vary, but almost all classification schemes include or imply the general areas of planning, integrating, coordinating, organizing, and controlling. Decision making is a function that cuts across all management activities, but often is studied separately. Part of the conventional wisdom is that routine decisions are controlled by the manager but made by others, and that nonroutine or critical decisions are reserved for managers. If, on occasion, a manager is caught muddling through an important decision, it can be inferred from the foregoing that he or she does it with aplomb.

Regardless of the different terms used to describe them, the functions that seem to distinguish management positions from others in the organization are those related to keeping the organization together (the "glue" function), giving it purpose and direction, coordinating the various subparts, ensuring that it meets its objectives effectively, acquiring resources from the external environment, keeping that environment as nourishing and predictable as possible, and creating buffers as needed to protect the organization against threats from the outside. These functions are usually considered as special prerogatives attached to positions or groups of positions whose incumbents are called on to "manage" rather than to "do."

Efforts to discover empirically what managers *do* have in some cases added significant detail to the list of functions, thus improving rather than disproving the classical POSDCORB, which still prevails in modified form in many texts and training courses. To some extent, this research has "demythologized" the vague, grandiose images of managers, and we know more about the process by which managers carry out their work, how they perceive it, and how some private and public sector managers spend their time. It has been shown that managers deal in and with ambiguity, cope with fragmented activities, favor personal contacts and odds and ends of information rather than reading to obtain aggregated information, work very hard, and do not perceive themselves as having enough time to devote to leadership and long-range planning for the organization. However, the sense that managers are supremely important to organizations prevails in both the empirical and the general literature.

The image of a manager as an individual who performs extraordinary and indispensible functions has been firmly established and well communicated by the literature to managers, students, and theorists in both the public and private sectors. Doubtless, there are managers who live up to or surpass their literary legacy. However, the tendency to glorify the role of manager creates a problem in that it makes more difficult any changes that threaten that role. The spirit of what has been written tends to create a cover of immutable sanctity for managers.

The profile of the *ideal* manager developed here will be compared with additional evidence available about what *real* managers do. For example, there are indications that our public managers spend more of their time on routine maintenance functions than on the more glamourous tasks often described in the literature, such as setting goals and giving leadership and direction to their respective organizations. This gap between idealized expectation and actual function will be discussed next.

CHAPTER 2

THE MAINTENANCE AND DEVELOPMENT FUNCTIONS OF MANAGERS

> *All I can really do around here is pass along the latest regulations from headquarters and see that my people follow them.*
>
> —A middle manager in a large county department

From the preceding sample of the traditional views that tend to aggrandize management, it is apparent that managers are expected to engage in activities that have as their main objective the change, adjustment, coordination, or improvement of the organization and of the environment surrounding the organization. Activities that are less likely to fit the image are those that have as their main objectives the perpetuation of existing procedures and resources within the organization. Various categories have been used by others to dichotomize the functions of managers with the same basic ideas in mind. These include routine and nonroutine, technical and conceptual, and administrative management and leadership.

Two similar categories, maintenance and development, were used in a survey designed to find out what public managers do (Martin, 1981). The results suggest that the managers surveyed do not live up to the model or image presented in the literature, and that there is an important gap between expectations held for managers and the experience of managers.

> ***Proposition 2:*** Managers more frequently engage in routine maintenance functions than they do in conceptualizing problems and opportunities or in planning for the development of the organization.

SURVEY FINDINGS

During 1979, managers from city, state, and federal agencies participated in a survey designed to find out more about what public managers do. (Background notes on the survey can be found in Appendix A.) They were asked to estimate on a questionnaire the percentage of their time during the preceding year spent on the broad functional areas of maintenance and development:

> The work of managers may be categorized according to whether the primary purpose of an activity is to *maintain* the organization or to *develop* or *change* the organization. Please estimate the percentage of time you spent during the past year on activities that were essentially maintenance and the percentage on those that were essentially development activities.

The composite manager (combining all levels of management) estimated that 37 percent of his or her time was spent on development as opposed to 63 percent on maintenance. (A summary of the responses of all managers to all questionnaire items is shown in Appendix B.)

Eight of the more specific activities listed on the questionnaire were grouped for purposes of analysis according to whether they were predominantly maintenance or developmental in nature. The mean response of managers from all levels who were considered to be "part of management" is shown in Table 2.1

TABLE 2.1 Selected Functions and Activities of Managers Clustered Under Development or Maintenance

Development	Mean Frequency[a]		Maintenance
Policy development (181)	4.5	6.1	Policy implementation (180)
Contacts with other government agencies (182)	3.8	7.5	Contacts with subordinates (181)
Contacts with policy, legislative, advisory, or regulatory bodies (180)	3.1	6.6	Supervision (182)
Conflict resolution (181)	4.2	6.2	Routine paperwork (182)

NOTE: The labels or terms used in each cluster are taken verbatim from the questionnaire. The numbers in parentheses indicate the number of managers who responded to the item. Instructions to respondents were: Please estimate the frequency with which you have dealt with the activities listed during the past year.
a. The scale provided was 1 = not at all; 9 = very frequent.

It can be argued that the activities listed do not fall neatly and permanently in either of the two broad categories. However, dozens of conversations, interviews, and pretests suggest that the division of activities as shown reflects the experience of most managers most of the time. For example, contacts with subordinates and supervision may have many diverse purposes, but they are more likely to involve exchanges of information in the interests of maintaining or controlling resources and individual or group performance than they are to involve the planning of broad organizational change and improvement.

As might be expected, top management had a profile different from that of lower levels of managers. Table 2.2 summarizes the differences in the responses received.

The figures shown in Table 2.2 labeled "frequency of occurrence" were obtained by computing for the two management levels the overall mean response to the question of the frequency of occurrence of the activities shown in Table 2.1. The essential relationship of development to maintenance remained the same (the former being less frequent or absorbing a smaller

TABLE 2.2 Overall Comparison of Extent to Which Top Managers and Other Managers Engage in Development and Maintenance Activities

	Top Managers (N = 44)	
	Development	Maintenance
Mean % of time	45%	54%
Mean frequency of occurrence of specific activities	4.6	5.9

	Other Managers (N = 138)	
	Development	Maintenance
Mean % of time	33%	66%
Mean frequency of occurrence of specific activities	3.6	6.8

NOTE: The frequency scale used by respondents was from 1 = not at all to 9 = very frequent.

percentage of time than the latter) when either the broad categories of maintenance and development, or the more specific uncategorized activities, were being considered by respondents. This consistency adds a degree of confidence to the ways in which the specific activities were grouped in Table 2.1.

The traditional management view is that activities in organizations should be divided in such a way that the higher-salaried managers engage in the nonroutine planning and developmental kinds of activities and avoid engaging in the routine maintenance kinds of activities. However, the manager profile emerging from this survey suggests otherwise, thus supporting the proposition that there is a gap between the activities befit-

interesting and rewarding. However, the desire for less maintenance and more development has probably also been fostered by expectations expressed by the managers' superordinates or subordinates, by their occasional exposure to management training courses, by their formal education or general acculturation, or by reading the management literature.

SIMILARITIES OF PUBLIC AND BUSINESS SECTORS

It is interesting to note that although the aggrandizement of managers has been accomplished primarily through the writing of those concerned with the private sector, it has influenced the education and training of those in public administration. When the reading habits of 191 practitioners and 144 academicians in public administration were studied, it was found that these two groups have been greatly influenced by the same five books (Bowman, 1978, p. 565): Simon's *Administrative Behavior* (1976), Barnard's *The Functions of the Executive* (1938/1954), McGregor's *The Human Side of Enterprise* (1960), Drucker's *The Practice of Management* (1954), and Taylor's *The Principles of Scientific Management* (1911/1934). The point of interest for our purposes (although not the purpose of the study) is that all of these books, with the possible exception of Simon's, were written from a business or industrial perspective.

It seems unlikely that the image of the ideal manager, created primarily with the problems of the business world in mind, will lose its ability to influence public managers, particularly in light of the steady convergence of the two sectors. Schools of public and business administration or management are continuing to combine within universities; management training courses are less likely now than in the past to be offered exclusively either for business or for public managers; and, as previously pointed out, books on management generally include managers from all kinds of organizations among their intended readers. Also, the nature of the work itself promotes a convergence:

> As things stand, a fairly straight-forward business management approach is probably appropriate for a large number of government activities. The management problems involved in mail delivery, defense logistics, hospital administration, highway construction, electric power generation and similar activities are problems amenable to the technical and managerial style embodied by the business approach [McCurdy, 1978, p. 577].

McCurdy points out that in 1976, public sector activities in which tendencies toward business management are most pronounced numbered 13 and involved 4,832,000 state and local personnel (p. 576).

Another factor to be considered is that as state and local jurisdictions attempt to maintain government services in the face of declining resources, they are giving more attention to the possibilities of various kinds of partnerships with profit-making organizations (or of themselves engaging in profit-making activities).

These are just a few of the indications of increased similarity and interactions between the public and private sectors. One item of difference, particularly relevant to this study and discussed in greater depth later, is that although the public sector has borrowed the aggrandizement of management for much the same reasons the private sector has found it useful, it has largely failed to borrow the work redesign efforts in private business that have posed a serious challenge to the supremacy and indispensability of a special group of people called managers.

Summary

Do public managers fulfill the image of the ideal manager, one who is a conceptualizer, who directs or leads his or her organization, who deals with the external environment, and who engages in long-range planning and policymaking? The answer proposed in this chapter is, at best, "occasionally."

The composite public manager surveyed with regard to the distribution of his or her activities within maintenance or development categories turns out to be approximately two-thirds maintainer and only one-third developer. Moreover, managers are generally dissatisfied with the way they spend their time, preferring more development and less maintenance involvement. As would be expected, top managers surveyed tend to be closer to the ideal than are lower-level managers, but still report spending more time on maintenance than on development. The image of manager as developer persists, largely a creation of those who have written about business leaders, but whose writings have greatly influenced both practitioners and academicians in the field of public administration.

Three factors related to the content of this chapter will continue to concern us in subsequent chapters: (1) The very real need for direction and conceptual ability from a few people in public organizations has been expanded to an imagined need for increasing numbers of people at all levels called managers. (2) Many of those paid to do the special work of managers do not actually perform these functions; instead, they perform maintenance functions, some of which (it will be proposed) are unneeded. (3) The numbers of such positions held by individuals who are not performing the important functions expected of them add greatly to the cost of the government workforce.

In the first part of the next chapter, we will consider a phenomenon that helps to sustain the popular perception that managers are indispensable to their subordinates and to the performance of the organization as a whole: the separation of managing from doing. The second section will be devoted to an examination of what has been called "average grade escalation" and of some of the existing ratios of superordinates to subordinates.

CHAPTER 3

THE MANAGING/DOING DICHOTOMY

> *Work is of two kinds: first, altering the position of matter at or near the earth's surface relative to other such matter; second, telling other people to do so. The first kind is unpleasant and ill paid; the second is pleasant and highly paid.*
>
> —Bertrand Russell

The admonition to managers against "doing" and in favor of "managing" (or as sometimes expressed, "getting the work done through others") is both popular and durable. It is also expensive, and those who wish to reduce the costs of government need to reexamine this familiar adage. The time is right for consideration of the cost involved when so many people in government seem to spend so much of their time "telling other people to do so."

The word "manage" means to direct or control the use of, to handle, wield, or use; it comes from the Latin word, *manus,* meaning hand. The Italian, *maneggiare,* means to handle, particularly in connection with training a horse in its paces. Looking beyond these rather humble origins, James Burnham predicted that at the end of the transition period from a capitalist or bourgeois to a managerial society, "The managers will, in fact, have achieved social dominance, will be the ruling class in society" (1941/1960, p. 72). Having such a wide and confusing range of possible identities, it is not surprising that managers can occasionally be observed behaving as hands-on rulers who enjoy putting employees through their paces.

The formal separation of managing from doing, and manager from worker, is one of the most enduring characteristics of organizations. The distinction of interest is between those who primarily apply their labor directly to an organizational product or service, and those who primarily organize, direct, or control the labor of others. In this section, we will examine the origins of the dichotomy, and present evidence and ideas in support of the following proposition:

> ***Proposition 3:*** The managing/doing dichotomy, or the separation of conception from execution, serves to keep the labor process dependent on management, thus ensuring the continued importance of a group of people called managers.

Origins and Nature of the Dichotomy

According to Braverman (1974), the separation of the conception of work from the execution of work coincided with the needs of evolving forms of capitalism. He describes how, in the early days of mercantile capitalism, the worker and his or her trade skills were hired, or subcontracted, but kept intact. This was common until the mid-nineteenth century. During the ensuing 100 years, with changing modes of production available, capitalists invented a new social relationship of workers to task, in which they brought workers together under one roof to take advantage of production technology, to better control workers, and to facilitate the division of labor into its simplest, cheapest, and most interchangeable parts.

Braverman believes that work and workers are systematically degraded under capitalistic systems, and that the situation is due to the thinking and influence of Frederick Taylor, more than to any other single person. He saw no sign (in 1974) of the diminishing influence of Taylor and the principles of scientific management, in part because of what he views as a symbiotic relationship between "Taylorism" and the human relations movement:

> The successors to Taylor are to be found in engineering and work design, and in top management; the successors to Münsterberg and Mayo are to be found in personnel departments and schools of industrial psychology and sociology. Work itself is organized according to Taylorian principles, while personnel departments and academics have busied themselves with the selection, training, manipulation, pacification, and adjustment of "manpower" to suit the work processes so organized. Taylorism dominates the world of production; the practitioners of "human relations" and "industrial psychology" are the maintenance crew for the human machinery [Braverman, 1974, p. 87].

SCIENTIFIC MANAGEMENT

Since Taylor's thinking has been instrumental in the separation of managing from doing, or conception from execution, it is worth examining in more detail. After clarifying the differences between (1) the former system of management in which workers have responsibility for planning their work and for selection and care of their implements, and (2) the use of the new science in which rules, laws, and formulas replace the workers' judgment, Taylor notes that the paraphernalia for all these scientific data require a room, desk, and books, and concludes as follows:

> Thus all of the planning which under the old system was done by the workman . . . must of necessity under the new system be done by the management in accordance with the laws of the science; because even if the workman was well suited to the development and use of scientific data, it would be physically impossible for him to work at his machine and at a desk at the same time. It is also clear that in most cases, one type of man is needed to plan ahead and an entirely different type to execute the work [Taylor, 1911/1934, p. 38].

Three "principles" of scientific management that have survived and continue to guide modern management are summarized by Braverman: (1) gathering and developing knowledge of the labor process, and dissociating the labor process from the skills of the workers; (2) concentrating this knowledge as exclusive to management (specifically keeping it from the workers); and (3) using the monopoly over knowledge to control each step in the labor process and its mode of execution (pp. 112-119).

The cleavage between managing and doing, or conception and execution has a long history, and it is still favored, with some modifications, by many writers and practitioners. Taking what appears to be an enlightened position with regard to integrated jobs, Drucker argues that each job should embody some element of skill or judgment; however, he reaches the more conventional conclusion that "even the lowliest human job should have some planning; only it should be simple planning and there should not be too much of it" (Drucker, 1954, p. 296).

The principles of Frederick Taylor are very much a part of public management. Efforts to become more efficient, effective, and "scientific" are common in public organizations; approaches such as those involving job analysis, task specialization, and the separation of conception from execution are well known. This is not surprising when considering that, as reported earlier, many activities in public organizations are judged to be quite businesslike (McCurdy, 1978), and the training and education of managers is less and less differentiated. As the nongovernment sector becomes increasingly more service producing than goods producing, the opportunities for utilizing similar management techniques in both public and private enterprises increases. Also, most occupations in the United States are common to both sectors. From a list of 426 occupations appearing on printouts obtained from the Department of Labor (December 1980), 92 could be identified as "private sector only," and about 14 as public sector, but the vast majority of occupations (321) are found in both.

Therefore, with a similar heritage and with similar kinds of workers, the explanation of Braverman about the origins of the managing/doing dichotomy in the private sector is relevant to our understanding of the public sector. Scientific management principles tend to encourage methods of task specialization, routinization, and the assignment of people to fragmented rather than to whole tasks. These methods accomplish the objective that Braverman and others deplore: Knowledge of the overall labor process remains the exclusive property of management; the worker remains dependent, and the need for supervision of these dependents is assured.

It seems unlikely that the separation of managing from doing has been a conscious plot; rather, it is more likely that the requirements of capitalist production, combined with the similar interests of existing or aspiring managers, academicians, civil service commissions, personnel specialists, those who assume the incompetence of workers, and those who assert the necessity of a vertical career ladder, form a natural alliance in perpetuating a group of persons called managers. By describing roles and tasks in such a way that the control and overall knowledge of the work performed by the organization are reserved for one group, the management role is assured.

BUREAUCRATIC CONTROL

Another view of the evolution of the control of workers by capitalist managers is presented by Edwards, who describes how industrial firms have utilized bureaucratic controls. This development had much in common with the earlier successful utilization of technical control, which was often embedded in the technological requirements of production and built into the plant architecture, the design and location of tools and machines, and other aspects of the physical layout. Control of this kind was seen as more effective than that exercised personally by the foreman on the shop floor, just as bureaucratic control was judged more effective than that exercised personally by a superordinate anywhere in the organization. The use of bureaucratic controls tends to institutionalize "the exercise of hierarchical power within the firm. The definition and direction of work tasks, the evaluation of worker performances, and the distribution of rewards and imposition of punishment all came to depend upon established rules and procedures, elaborately and systematically laid out" (Edwards, 1979, p. 131).

Whether the setting is industry, business, or government, many of the implications of the substitution of bureaucratic control for personal interactions have been dealt with at great length in the literature on bureaucracy. One implication for the public sector that is not usually considered, however, will be addressed in more detail in subsequent chapters. At this point, it will merely be identified: With the abundance of comprehensive, detailed rules governing the behavior of public employees, the need for a virtual army of middle and lower-level managers to offer essentially redundant control over subordinates deserves to be questioned.

Changes in Superordinate to Subordinate Ratios

While not everyone will agree with the foregoing version of the evolution of the manager's role, most do agree that it is important to consider the relative numbers of those who manage, administer, or supervise, and those who produce, and the changes in that ratio over time. C. Northcote Parkinson (1957/1978) speaks to this issue with humor.

> We must picture a civil servant, called A, who finds himself overworked. Whether this overwork is real or imaginary is immaterial, but we should observe, in passing, that A's sensation (or illusion) might easily result from his own decreasing energy: a normal symptom of middle age. For this real or imagined overwork there are, broadly speaking, three possible remedies. He may resign; he may ask to halve the work with a colleague called B; he may demand the assistance of two subordinates, to be called C and D. There is probably no instance in history, however, of A choosing any but the third alternative [p. 195].

Parkinson notes that very soon after implementing the third alternative, two assistants are assigned to C and D, and seven officials are doing the work one did before. "For these seven make so much work for each other that all are fully occupied and A is actually working harder than ever" (Parkinson, 1957/1978, p. 195). Later in the article, he presents evidence (and a formula) to substantiate his estimates of the growth rate of what he calls the staff or administration of various organizations compared with the work or output of those organizations. "Dealing with the problems of pure staff accumulation, all our researches so far completed point to an average increase of 5.75 per cent per year" (p. 197), and this he adds is "irrespective of any variation in the amount of work (if any) to be done" (p. 198).

The story of Civil Servant A, his sense of overwork, the solution he chooses, and the consequences of that choice, is one way of accounting for the "rising pyramid." Some observers (who might consider themselves more modern and less cynical) are likely to attribute growth in the numbers of levels, as well as the increasing numbers of positions at higher levels, to the growing complexity of the work itself, which in turn is a product of a complex environment full of multiple constraints and demands.

Using Polaroid as an example, Edwards examines stratification as a mechanism for control, observing that the firm's system of control is built on a "finely graded division and stratification of workers," which has the effect of breaking up "the homogeneity of the firm's workforce, creating many seemingly separate strata, lines of work, and focuses for job identity" (1979, p. 133). "One important consequence of this new stratification has been the rapidly growing number of employees who supervise other workers, not only at Polaroid but elsewhere as well" (p. 135). Edwards notes that there has been a steady growth in the number of foremen per 100 workers in manufacturing companies from 1910 to 1970; there was a 67 percent increase during the period from 1940 to 1970, compared with a mere 15 percent increase between 1910 and 1940 (p. 135).

Much of the increase in the total workforce of the United States, according to the U.S. Bureau of Labor Statistics, is attributable to a group usually labeled "professional and technical" whose ranks have increased dramatically. They represented 11.4 percent of the total workforce in 1960 and 16.1 percent in 1980, and grew in actual numbers from 7,469,000 in 1960 to 15,613,000 in 1980, an increase of 109 percent. By comparison, sales workers, clerical workers, craft workers, operatives, nonfarm laborers, and service workers together increased in the same period from 46,066,000 to 68,034,000, a 47.7 percent increase. "Managers and administrators" were 7,067,000 in number in 1960 (10.7 percent of the total workforce) and 10,026,000 in 1980 (11.2 percent of the total workforce), an increase of 41.9 percent (Statistical Abstract, 1981, p. 401). While the numbers of managers and administrators had a growth rate lower than that of professional and technical personnel (as well as being significantly fewer in absolute numbers by 1980), it is not known how many of the latter occupy supervisorial positions within organizations or are considered "part of management."

Comparing the familiar categories of white-collar and blue-collar workers, the former was estimated at 28,522,000 for the United States as a whole in 1960 and 50,809,000 in 1980, an increase of 78 percent. The blue-collar workforce was 24,057,000 in 1960 and 30,800,000 in 1980, an increase of 28 percent (Statistical Abstract, 1981, p. 401). Within the federal government, a similar trend can be noted. In 1968, 70 percent of the civilian workers in the federal government were white-collar compared with 30 percent who were blue-collar workers, and in 1978, the percentages were 76 percent and 24 percent, respectively (U.S. Officer of Personnel Management, 1980, p.6).

As stated earlier, additions to the workforce at the higher grade levels (such as the dramatic growth in professional and technical personnel) may include some positions that are supervisory and others that are not, which means that we do not know from these data alone how many people are telling others to "do so." Similarly, the growth in the numbers of white-collar compared with blue-collar workers may or may not indicate an increase in the numbers of supervisory positions. However, additional data on grade escalation and span of control in public-sector organizations have been found that lend credence to the claim that there are unnecessary management or supervisorial positions in some government organizations. These data will be presented following Proposition 4, which provides a context in which to consider them:

> *Proposition 4:* Average grade escalation and narrow spans of control intensify the need for experimenting with alternatives to the managing/doing dichotomy.

It is important to note the word "intensifies" in this proposition. With or without grade escalation, there is a need for such experimentation. The evidence to be presented in this section is intended to stimulate interest in the need for a change, an interest that might not exist if all of our public agencies were actively reducing the upper and middle ranks of management and the levels of supervision. Unfortunately, government bureaucracies, with some exceptions, appear to be adapting to this era of scarce resources simply by maintaining less populous hierarchies, trimmer at the bottom, but with "fat" in the upper middle region.

GRADE ESCALATION

When the General Accounting Office (GAO) recently took a look at the Department of Defense (DOD), it pointed out that although there was an average grade increase from 7.29 in 1964 to 7.58 in 1974, and 7.89 in 1980, it was a smaller increase (as well as a lower average grade) than occurred for all General Service (GS) employees in non-DOD agencies. These changes in DOD occurred while the total personnel in that department went from 522,937 in 1964 to 608,868 in 1974, and dropped to 570,806 in 1980 (GAO, 1981, p. 36).

Although DOD experienced a rather mild grade escalation and is a unique organizational entity with very specialized and technical functions, the possible reasons advanced for the changes in grade distribution are worth reviewing for their applicability to other areas of government. The first general explanation in the report cited was that the advanced technology and increasing complexity of defense work required a more professional, technically oriented workforce such as highly graded scientists, engineers, economists, lawyers, analysts, and computer specialists.

Other possible causes were grouped together under personnel policies and organizational factors. Some of those listed as contributing to grade escalation were: (1) hiring restrictions on entry-level positions, (2) career ladder promotions, (3) higher attrition in lower grades, (4) staffing patterns required for a mix of civilian, military, and contract personnel, (5) consolidation and mission changes that result in decreased need for support personnel (lower grades), and (6) contracting out the less complex and lower graded work (pp. 13-17).

Other "interdependent" factors listed included automation, which has replaced lower-graded clerical and administrative personnel with advanced electronic equipment, which in turn requires higher-graded professional and technical personnel; material sophistication (modern weapon systems have in many cases replaced large combat forces); demographics of a better-educated and trained workforce; and competition with the private sector (p. 18).

The last mentioned factor was that of "unwarranted grade growth." (In general, the report found more warranted than unwarranted grade growth.) "Despite the fact that much of the grade escalation since 1964 may be justified by the reasons discussed above, some management practices can produce grade escalation which is not justified" (p. 18). The practices mentioned were inflated position descriptions, supervisory layering, job dilution, narrow spans of control, and unwarranted use of assistants and deputies. The report concludes that "the central issue in arguments about grade escalation is whether or not the explanations advanced for it do in fact justify its occurrence. Average grade is only a gross measure of changes in employee distribution and cannot indicate whether these changes are justified or cost effective" (p. 32). However, the budgetary importance of grade control mechanisms was not overlooked; it was estimated that even a "small amount of grade growth can cost an organization the size of DOD several million dollars annually" (p. 33).

In the DOD example, the management practices that produce the least justifiable grade escalation would seem to be the most "correctable." Such reforms are frequently (and unfortunately) left in the hands of the managers who necessitated them. The conclusion reached by the GAO is that it is necessary to guard against unwarranted grade escalation by congressional oversight. The report recommends that the secretary of defense insure that each DOD component complies with position management guidelines, and that deficiencies in this regard become part of performance appraisals. They also urge Congress, during oversight hearings, to require components to report on the adequacy of position management programs.

Within the federal government as a whole (non-DOD), grade escalation is ore pronounced than in the DOD. Average grade rose from 7.63 in 1964 to 8.35 in 1980, while the total number of GS employees grew from 579,264 to 831,414. The lower grades (GS 1, 2, and 3) and the top grades (GS 16, 17, and 18) all showed a decline, while the greatest single increase (120.1 percent) occurred in grade 14. There were also large increases in grades 10, 12, 13, and 15 (GAO Report, 1980, p. 35). These figures reinforce the image of a hierarchy that "bulges" in the upper middle, rather than at the top or the bottom.

In studying the fiscal containment of local and state government, a group from Rand did a special study of budget increases in the City of Los Angeles during the period from 1973 to 1978.

> Inflation (in compensation and other expenditures together) accounts for three-quarters of the increase, and 'upward float' in employee compensation another 11 percent. We determined that, during the five-year study period, there has been a gradual

shift in the mix of city employees in Los Angeles, with a decrease in the number of regular employees in direct service functions and an increase in the number in support and administrative functions. This shift is evidenced not only by a relative increase in size and budget of overhead agencies as compared with direct service agencies, but also by a reorientation of expenditures within agencies toward the administrative functions. This shift further increased the cost of government because the added personnel in support functions have higher salaries and faster rates of increase in benefits than did the direct service personnel they replaced [Pascal, Menchik, Chaiken, Ellickson, Walker, DeTray, & Wise, 1979, p. 54].

The authors conclude that there is no easy solution to this problem; some of the added administrative functions are designed for increased efficiency of the direct service providers or for meeting federal and state mandates, and, if successful in meeting these objectives, eliminating the functions might have unwanted effects.

A recent effort to change the structure of the Los Angeles Police Department reflects concern with the "upward float" syndrome. Figures from the City Administrative Office indicate that since 1970, the number of officers increased by 3 percent, while in the same period the number of senior officers increased by 36 percent. On January 26, 1982, the city council passed a resolution to phase out 18 top positions with the original intent of "allowing" the department to hire 107 patrol officers. However, an amendment was passed that reserved for the chief of police the freedom to reorganize the department in any way, just as long as the savings (estimated at $3.5 million annually) and the elimination of the top positions were accomplished; in fact, the savings might not be used to hire additional officers but to offset anticipated budget cuts in the future. In any case, even after mandated cuts have been made, "Police brass will be up 94% since 1950, more than double the rate of increase in patrol officers and detectives" (Johnston, 1982).

Personal forays into some of the small- or medium-sized cities in Southern California to learn about changes over time in the superordinate-to-subordinate ratio produced few results, except an invitation to sort through yearly budgets for possible clues. This proved to be a formidable task; changing position titles and budget formats made comparisons over time very difficult. However, a general impression gained from these efforts is that the small- and medium-sized cities tend to be lean rather than fat. They appear to be less "top heavy" than larger jurisdictions, even though some of them have made significant increases (sometimes disproportionate to increases in other position categories) in the numbers of "professional and technical" positions. When the increases are discussed, they are attributed to the need for personnel to handle special projects requiring technical expertise. (In spite of these reasonable explanations, it is not at all unusual to hear complaints emanating from the line departments in some cities about the constant addition to "administration," while the size of their own workforce is diminishing.)

SPAN OF CONTROL

Span of control data, when available, have been the only direct evidence of the numbers of managers or supervisors overseeing the work done by their subordinates in a given organization or subunit. In a report by the Task Force on Management and Finances of the Los Angeles County Economy and Efficiency Commission (1976, pp. 24-31), the ratio of supervisors to subordinates was examined. The procedure used was to examine data from the Auditor-Controller's Item Control Report. A given position was determined to be "supervisorial" by looking for key words and titles attached to each position. There were some positions that were not clearly supervisorial, and for these, several other criteria were applied, such as salary, position in the classification hierarchy, and others.

The task force found that supervisory salaries in fiscal 1975-1976 totaled approximately $190 million, and that averages from aggregated data show that the county "spends $25 on supervision for every $100 of subordinate salaries and employs one supervisor for each 5.8 subordinates" (p. 29). They speculate that if the $25 per $100 of subordinate salaries was reduced to $23, this would require the deletion of approximately 700 supervisory positions and would yield an annual savings to the county of $13 million.

A conclusion reached by the task force is that further study by the CAO is necessary. "The County appears to us to have too many supervisory positions. As many as 15 departments have supervisory ratios of 20% or more—that is one or more supervisors for each five subordinates. While such levels may be justified in special circumstances and may be common in the public sector, we are convinced that in many cases they represent a major departure from reasonable standards of control" (pp. 7-8). In another section of the report (p. 24), actual levels in some departments were cited as being as high as one supervisor for every two or three subordinates.

The report includes mention of the nonmonetary benefits of improving the ratios of supervisor to subordinate. "Over-supervision has damaging effects beyond the problem of cost. Communication deteriorates. Too many levels of supervision between operating personnel and management cause delay and distortion of information in both directions. As a consequence, morale and the incentive to perform decline" (p. 9).

Data from the office of the Chief Administrative Officer of Los Angeles County in August 1978 showed an average ratio of managers and supervisors to all positions (which include managers and supervisors) to be 1 supervisor to 7 "subordinates," with a range of 1:4 to 1:15, and improvement over the average 1:5.8 ratio reported by the task force. The claim was made that the numbers of managers and supervisors are within reasonable personnel management standards; the conclusions in the report by the task force of the Economy and Efficiency Commission were specifically refuted, but the importance of continuing efforts to control the ratios was acknowledged.

Few believe that a particular and "correct" span of control exists independently of situational elements such as the functions being performed, the experience and abilities of the workers, the technicality of the work, and the competence of the supervisor. However, complete analyses in which all such relevant factors are considered on a case-by-case basis are expensive and time consuming, particularly in large organizations. Some organizations apparently neither strive for uniform spans nor perform a case-by-case analysis; the previous year's span is frequently used as a guideline when positions are being filled in any given unit. Based on personal experience, records of changes in the ratios over time are either not kept at all or are not readily available in many organizations and must be inferred from data collected for other purposes. (Los Angeles County was an exception in that regard.)

When span of supervision data are available, they are often presented in the form of "average ratios," or as budgeted rather than actual ratios, either of which may serve to obscure important specific incidences of abuse. On those relatively rare occasions when systematic efforts are initiated to decide the appropriate span in a particular situation, too often the scope of the analyses is as narrow as some of the spans; managers tend to limit themselves to consideration of alternatives that can exist comfortably within the framework of existing numbers of employees at existing levels in the organization, and to alternatives that are based on traditional views about the necessity of supervision. This approach tends to forestall arguments as to whether or not supervision or control is needed at all.

In the case of Los Angeles County, it is apparent that with conflicting claims, diverse methods of acquiring and analyzing data, and differences between budgeted and actual ratios, no firm conclusions can be drawn about the changes in the ratio of managers and supervisors to other employees over time, much less about the appropriateness of the various spans. If, as claimed, the average span widened in two years from 1:5.8 to 1:7, this is a noteworthy achievement; within an organization with a traditional structure and a conservative management, it may be necessary to welcome (as one step toward reduced supervision), any efforts to widen the spans of control.

All things considered, it appears likely that a number of unnecessarily narrow spans still exist in the County of Los Angeles; management practices such as those mentioned in the GAO's report on the DOD (inflated position descriptions, supervisory layering, job dilution, and unwarranted use of assistants and deputies) can undoubtedly be found there, as in any large bureaucracy. It should be emphasized, as it was in the commission's report and in the report on the DOD, that the deletion of any unnecessary levels of supervision, particularly in large systems, would represent substantial savings.

It is tempting to charge that all public organizations are top heavy or "fat." However, everyone can cite exceptions to that charge. More important, there is great difficulty in generalizing about what is indeed top heavy, and what is indispensable for carrying on the work at hand. Specific organizations and subunits within them may be aware of whether the charge for them is true. However, there are endless ways of rationalizing existing hierarchies, and there is a natural reluctance to consider either oneself or one's colleagues to be too highly graded. As a result, any awareness of abuse is seldom made explicit.

Many signs point to the increasingly important role of state governments as the New Federalism gets underway. Increased attention will doubtless be given to the costs of state government, and data from the State of California on the ratio of superordinates to subordinates are not particularly reassuring in this regard. In the annual census of state employees in 1975, 1978, and 1981 provided by the State Personnel Board, there is a breakdown of supervisory and nonsupervisory positions. Some of these are shown in Table 3.1.

Conclusions about these figures must be tentative. Specific knowledge about who supervises whom, how many, and why, would be needed in order to proceed with an analysis. However, based solely on the aggregate data shown, there appears to be a remarkably narrow span of control in many job categories in the state government in California. The broadest span (not shown in the table) was in the category labeled "law,"

TABLE 3.1 Selected Full-Time State Civil Service Employees by Job Category

	1975	1978	1981
Professional	16,689	16,633	18,107
Supervising Professional	10,572	8,808	9,044
Ratio of supervisor to subordinates*	1:1.6	1:1.9	1:2
Field Representative	2,612	2,475	2,575
Supervising Field Rep.	1,926	2,134	1,834
Ratio of supervisor to subordinates*	1:1.4	1:1.2	1:1.4
Administrative Staff	2,764	10,190	9,566
Admin. Staff–Supervising	1,091	3,557	4,460
Ratio of supervisor to subordinates*	1:2.5	1:2.9	1:2.1

SOURCE: Adapted from the Annual Census of State Employees of July 1975, 1978, and 1981, California State Personnel Board.
*The ratios were not shown in the census, but computed from the figures given.

which went from 1:1.8 in 1975 to 1:4.8 in 1978 and 1:4.7 in 1981. This latter figure was the broadest span computed for 1981, followed closely by the subprofessional/technical (1:4.6) and clerical (1:4.4) groups.

Quite apart from the scattered statistics that bear on narrow spans of control and on grade escalation, there is a "gut feeling" reported by many practitioners that the higher-level positions have proliferated relative to the lower levels, and that some degree of unnecessary supervision occurs. During periods of retrenchment, it is typically the "last hired" who is the "first fired." These individuals, more often than not, occupied positions low in the hierarchy. Also, it is a fairly common practice to grant promotions in order to hold good employees in otherwise dead-end jobs, to gain better bargaining positions with labor unions, or simply to "raise the morale of the troups." These practices tend to have the overall effect of raising the average grade level and, in some cases, adding to the "layers" of supervision.

Summary

The familiar warning to managers that they must manage rather than do has been reexamined in this chapter within the context of Taylor's principles of scientific management, which encourage the separation of conception from execution ("one type of man is needed to plan ahead and an entirely different type to execute the work"), specialization, routinization of tasks, and the assignment of people to fragmented rather than to whole tasks. These principles continue to influence the operations of many organizations today.

The need to experiment with alternatives to the managing/doing dichotomy is intensified by evidence of grade escalation and narrow spans of control in some public organizations. Upward grade float, or average grade escalation, has occurred in the federal government and in the city of Los Angeles. In themselves, these data do not "prove" a growing number of superordinates compared with subordinates since an indeterminate number of those hired at the higher grades supervise others. However, when the grade escalation figures are added to evidence of span-of-control abuses (reported and denied in Los Angeles County and appearing in aggregate data about supervisory and nonsupervisory job categories in the State of California), the growing numbers of supervisors per worker in manufacturing firms, the practice during budget cutbacks of firing the "last hired" who are usually those in lower-level positions, various management practices of inflated position descriptions, job dilution, and supervisory "layering," they combine to suggest an excess of management and supervisory positions.

In the following chapter, the question of whether or not subordinates feel they can do their work without supervision will be addressed.

CHAPTER 4

PERCEPTIONS OF SUPERVISION

> *We can do our work just fine
> without supervision. And anyway,
> supervisors are always in
> meetings and never around if
> we did need them.*
>
> —A state employee

Much like managers and management, supervision is rarely questioned in terms of its importance to the preservation and well-being of organizations and of the people who work in them. Many who may criticize particular kinds of supervision never doubt its importance as a function and continue to pursue "good" supervision (or supervisors). This unquestioning support would appear to be a natural consequence of the managing/doing dichotomy, which ensures the continued dependence of workers on someone called a manager or supervisor. Once the separation is contrived and the dependency instilled, it is difficult to question the importance of supervision.

However, there are a number of workers, who are, like the state employee quoted above, skeptical of the conventional wisdom. (The comment is taken verbatim from a questionnaire completed by an employee of the State of California who was participating in a survey about what managers do.) In this chapter, we will examine data indicating that many workers feel they can perform their work without supervision, as well as data indicating that many workers respond negatively to the prospect of not having a supervisor. The point will be made that, in spite of this ambivalence on the part of those being supervised and the reluctance on the part of managers and supervisors to entertain doubts about the positive influence of their oversight activities, the significance of supervision in achieving desired levels of performance has been greatly exaggerated.

Proposition 5: After an initial period of orientation and training, most individuals can perform their work without supervision.

The word supervise means to "direct and inspect the performance of (workers or work)." It is derived from Latin, *super* (over) *videre* (to see). This definition is usually considered too narrow by those who believe that managers and supervisors should be knowledgable in "human relations," and who prefer to expand supervision to include personal interactions with workers, in which the "growth" of the latter is facilitated. An opposing argument will be developed in more detail later in support of the belief that time spent by supervisors as counselors or "growth producers" for subordinates is largely unnecessary to the latter's well-being.

Supervision and Performance

In this chapter, attention will be focused on the proposition that time spent by superordinates in overseeing the activities of subordinates is, to a large extent, unnecessary to their performance. Since the two functions, human relations and oversight, are important components of the supervisor's job, a logical step (if one accepts the argument and the proposition) would be to reduce the amount of supervision. This reduction would save money as well as allow the supervisor to spend more time directly applying his or her labor to the service or product output of the organization.

CONTACTS WITH SUBORDINATES

In a 1979 survey of public employees categorized as managers and nonmanagers, several questions were asked about supervision (Martin, 1981). Two activities, supervision and contacts with subordinates, were perceived by managers in this survey as those in which they most frequently engage out of a possible eighteen activities listed. (The scale used was 1 = not at all frequent, and 9 = very frequent.) Contacts with subordinates received a mean rating of 7.5, and supervision a mean rating of 6.6 from 182 participating managers from city, state, and federal agencies.

In an earlier chapter, it was pointed out that the phrase "contacts with subordinates" is vague because such contacts are bound to occur for many different purposes, not all of which would necessarily be the checking, directing, or controlling of subordinates usually associated with routine supervision. However, impressions derived from over ten years of working closely with public organizations have led to some tentative conclusions about what "contacts with subordinates" are most likely to include and exclude. Such contacts are: (1) rarely of a collegial nature in which work problems are discussed, mutual input into the decision-making process encouraged, or long-range strategic plans generated; (2) occasionally for the purpose of evaluating the performance of the subordinate; and (3) frequently to give orders or instructions, or to reprimand the subordinate for some deficiency or delinquency in carrying out past directives. These tentative conclusions were reinforced by results from other portions of the same survey, and separate empirical studies have been congruent with this general theme. For example, Kurke and Aldrich (as noted in Chapter 1) found that managers' contacts with subordinates were for the purposes of making requests, sending or receiving information, and *occasionally* (my emphasis) strategy making (1979, p. 7).

The frequency ratings for the two items, supervision and contacts with subordinates, suggest that superordinates have an enormous time investment in what is essentially the control of subordinates. If, as proposed, the control and oversight aspects of supervision have been exaggerated in terms of their importance and may even be detrimental to effective performance, the amount of supervision (and the number of managers and supervisors) in any given organization should be closely scrutinized.

MANAGERS' INFLUENCE AND EFFECTS OF CHANGES IN SUPERVISION

In the same survey, managers were asked to rate the influence they had on the performance of subordinates (a mean of 7.1 on a 1-to-9 scale), and to estimate how various changes, such as more, less, or no supervision, might affect performance. The mean ratings on the latter item (how a change in supervision would affect performance) were generally low, with the highest, a mean of 4.0, given to "more supervision." The 154 participating nonmanagers estimated the influence of managers on their own performance as moderately high (5.7), while changes in supervision were perceived as having little or no influence on their own satisfaction, on the effectiveness of their work unit, or on the satisfaction of others. The only change that brought even slight improvement in either effectiveness or satisfaction was that of more supervision; all other changes brought overall slight to moderate decreases in satisfaction and effectiveness. The change viewed most negatively in its impact on unit effectiveness and others' satisfaction was "no supervisor"; the most negative impact on the responding nonmanagers' satisfaction was "additional supervisors." However, "no supervisor" was viewed as having the second most negative impact on the individual nonmanager's satisfaction. (Appendix D includes a table that summarizes these responses, and responses of nonmanagers to all survey items are summarized in Appendix C.)

COMPLETION OF ASSIGNMENTS WITHOUT SUPERVISION

The picture that emerges from these limited data is that the nonmanagers surveyed did not want more supervisors, but felt that their satisfaction would be negatively influenced if they had no supervisor at all. However, when work performance and supervision were linked in the following question ("How much of your present work assignment could you complete without

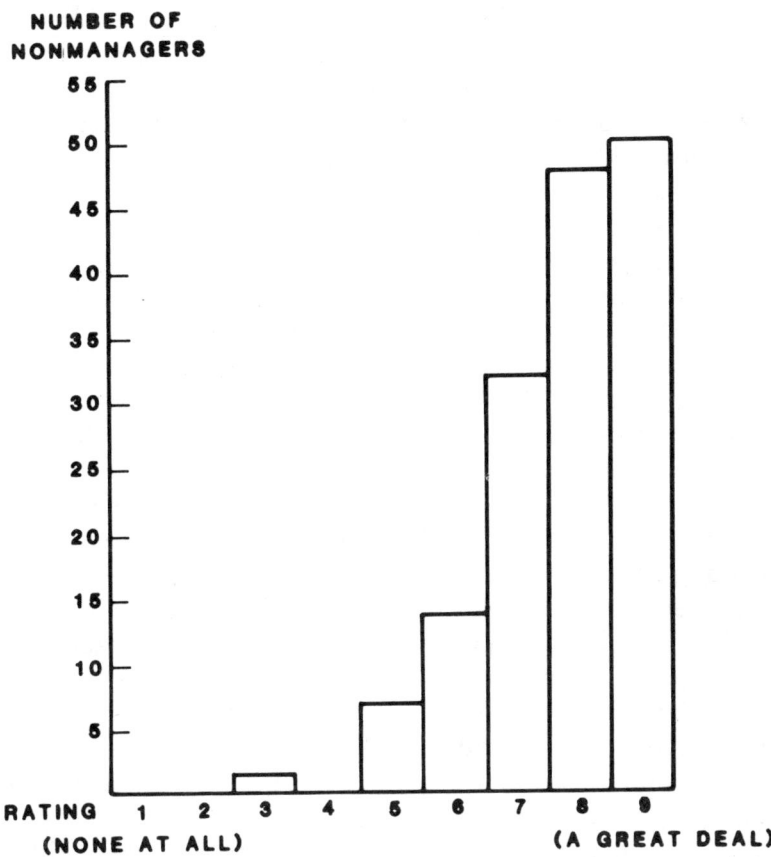

Figure 4.1 Distribution of Responses to the Question: "How much of your present work assignment could you complete without supervision?" (n = 154; Mean = 7.7)

supervision?"), the responses (as shown in Figure 4.1) are compelling.

Paradoxical Perceptions

On the face of it, the two categories of responses, "I would be more dissatisfied than satisfied with a change that would result in having no supervisor," and "I don't need to be supervised in order to perform my work," appear to be contradictory. On reflection, however, these responses on the part of nonmanagers may merely signal an understandable paradox. They, like others, have grown accustomed to the customary authority structures; their low *need* for supervision may seem to them to be unrelated to the continued existence of supervisors. More important, the existence of the position occupied by their supervisor represent for many subordinates a reminder of the possibility of their own advancement. The "career ladder" logic may not have been consciously employed at the time these questions were answered, but it seems reasonable to assume that subordinates who are interested in promotion are just as likely to impute importance to the superordinate's role as is the superordinate.

Ironically, the attitudes of subordinates may be as great an obstacle to consideration of changes in the numbers and functions of supervisors as are the attitudes of the supervisors or managers themselves. Experimentation with reductions in supervision is likely to be resisted by supervisors and managers for many reasons, one of which is that it represents a challenge to their pay and status as well as to their belief that workers must be directed and controlled; resistance on the part of subordinates may be based on a learned dependency on a supervisor or manager, an interest in being promoted, a genuine liking for their boss, fear of change, and other factors. However, within the context of the current harsh predictions of a future with continuing resource deficiencies, and of a public disenchanted with the size, cost, and effectiveness of government, the preferences of either supervisor or worker may simply have grown too expensive to be accommodated.

During studies of a city (Martin, 1978a) and a nursing department (Martin, 1979), there was a striking difference between written responses to specific items on a questionnaire about supervision (moderately positive), and the responses to open-ended items on the same questionnaire and the comments during interviews about supervisors (generally negative). There were 320 individuals participating from the city, and 790 from the nursing department, and all levels of the organizations were represented. (The nursing study included nurses only, but of varying rank.) In the written portions of both studies, a moderate degree of satisfaction with supervision was expressed. For example, when the individuals surveyed were asked about the extent of their satisfaction with the closeness of supervision (using a scale of 1 = very dissatisfied, and 7 = very satisfied), the mean rating in the city was 4.0 and the mean rating in the nursing department 4.8.

However, a different picture emerged during interviews and on the open-ended portions of the questionnaire. Some of the comments related to supervision written by city employees in response to an open-ended question about needed or desired changes were: more personal and humane treatment from supervisors, better supervisors who will "stand up" for employees, more authority and autonomy, more opportunity to plan work, and fewer supervisors.

During the group interviews with unskilled laborers, operatives, mechanics, and others in the city's maintenance and operations department and municipal utility department, the following kinds of comments were common:

> There is no coordination between the supervisor and the foreman in giving orders, so we frequently receive contradictory instructions.
>
> Yes-men are wanted here; only the bad stuff gets in your file, and when your name comes up for promotion, they (supervisors) use it against you.
>
> We think supervisors should be tested to see if they are fit to supervise others.
>
> Supervisors spend most of their time in meetings and spying on us. We do all the work; they shuffle papers.
>
> Our supervisors are incompetent; they are ignorant of the work, use bad judgment and make many mistakes.
>
> Supervisors do anything to make their section look good to upper management so they don't allow any complaints from workers.
>
> Supervisors act like cops and are always trying to bust you.

The nurses interviewed expressed similarly negative feelings; comments such as the following were expressed frequently in all sections of this large nursing organization:

> Supervisors don't know how to do the work and they don't know how to supervise either.
>
> Supervisors are untrustworthy.
>
> Supervisors give only negative feedback, and even that is rare.
>
> Supervisors are always in meetings and never available on the wards.

There are several plausible explanations as to why moderately positive responses would be elicited to specific written questions about supervision at the same time that generally negative comments predominated in the open-ended portions of the questionnaire and in interviews. The moderately high ratings on the questionnaire might be attributed to the recognition that supervision, as a step in the ladder, is necessary; to genuine appreciation on the part of subordinates for a helpful and possibly protective supervisor; to the lack of flexibility in the responses allowed, so that only those who had very strong and relatively uncomplicated negative feelings about supervision would give low ratings; to a general dislike of questionnaires, and a fear often expressed that even though no names were required, somehow the questionnaires could be traced to the individuals who completed them; or to socialization within the culture of organizations, which makes it difficult to imagine life at work without supervision.

On the other hand, when open-ended questions were asked on the questionnaire or space allowed for comments, respondents may have felt safer in expressing negative feelings in a way that allowed explanation of the context in which those feelings existed. Similarly, the informality of the group interviews (as well as the "us versus them" attitudes that occasionally were generated, and the possibility that respondents perceived subtle and, it should be added, unintended encouragement from the consultants) stimulated some individuals to *discuss* and elaborate on feelings of anger, disappointment, or dissatisfaction.

It is neither necessary nor possible to "prove" from these data that supervisors are liked or disliked, perceived as necessary or unnecessary, or that particular kinds of supervision receive high or low ratings from subordinates. It comes as no surprise that feelings, opinions, and attitudes about this important dimension of organizational life should be mixed. What is necessary to the theme of this study is to encourage acceptance of the possibility that regardless of fluctuating opinions and attitudes, most individuals can perform their work without supervision.

Another study of attitudes and behavior at work and how these related to gender, nationality, or ethnicity contributed some data of interest to the question of supervision (Martin, 1978b). A questionnaire was administered to 112 individuals from 17 different nations and 3 ethnic groups. There were 33 statements listed, and respondents were instructed to mark those statements that described their typical behavior at work and leave unmarked those statements that were not descriptive of their typical behavior at work. Of these 33 statements, 5 were related to supervision. These are listed below, along with the percentage of respondents who affirmed that particular behavior. The statements were preceded by, "At work, I usually . . .

(1) accept criticism from my supervisor without comment." (21 percent)
(2) work with a minimum of supervision." (88 percent)
(3) depend on my supervisor to check my work regularly." (19 percent)
(4) tell my supervisor when he or she makes a mistake that affects me." (64 percent)
(5) express to my supervisor my dissatisfaction or disagreement." (75 percent)

Item 2 above claimed the highest percentage of affirmative responses to any of the 33 items on the questionnaire. This result is congruent with the dramatic response give the public nonmanagers to the question, "How much of your present work assignment could you complete without supervision?" The answer given by 85 percent of the 154 nonmanagers participating was, in effect, "a great deal" (see Figure 4.1).

Summary

Data have been presented to lend support to the following description of supervision: (1) Supervision of subordinates consumes a large proportion of the time and energy of superordinates. (2) This supervision is largely unnecessary to the performance of work by subordinates. (3) Most subordinates do not want to work without a supervisor. A tentative conclusion is that, in spite of the ambivalence on the part of the subordinate, and in spite of the threat posed to the superordinate, the need for supervision in public organizations should be critically examined, and the incidence of supervision reduced whenever possible.

Cooperation as an alternative to supervision and control will be examined in the following chapter.

CHAPTER 5

COOPERATION UNDER THE "LAW OF THE SITUATION"

> *We shall always be seeking an external and arbitrary authority until we learn to direct our efforts toward seeking—the law of the situation.*
>
> —Mary Parker Follett

Some evidence has been presented to support the proposition that, to a large extent, subordinates can perform their tasks without supervision. However, the elimination or reduction of supervisory positions alone will surely not be sufficient to turn large, complex organizations into effective and less costly entities in which people enjoy a high quality of working life. In searching for a philosophy that will guide the invention of processes that can serve as alternatives to supervision and control, an "old" concept appears worthy of renewed exposure. It is the simple idea of cooperation. Two individuals, working and writing more than forty years ago, provide eloquent reminders of the importance of cooperation as a guiding force in organization. These are Chester Bernard and Mary Parker Follett.

Chester Barnard

Even though Chester Barnard was a traditionalist in many ways, his views on control set him apart. Barnard ardently believed in the importance of organizations in accomplishing society's purposes. He further believed that society's purposes are always moral, and that organizations are by nature cooperative efforts to achieve the purposes of society. When Barnard wrote *The Functions of the Executive* in 1938, he provided three main categories of essential executive functions: (1) to provide the system of communication, (2) to promote the securing of essential effort (e.g., maintenance of morale, maintenance of a scheme of inducements and deterrents, supervision and control, inspection, and training and education, and (3) to formulate and define purpose (1938/1954, pp. 217-234). His elaboration of the third major function is particularly relevant to the relationship of top management with others in the organization.

FORMULATION OF PURPOSE

Barnard explains that the purpose of the organization must be broken into fragments, or specific objectives, not just in time, but into specializations, such as geographical, social, and functional (p. 231). The purpose of the organization is defined more nearly by the aggregate of action taken than by any formulation of words, and it (the purpose) must be accepted by all the contributors to the system of efforts. An important aspect of the role of the executive (or top management) is the ability to provide "indispensable coordination. This requires a pyramiding of the formulation of purpose" (p. 232). Responsibility for abstract generalizing about prospective long-run decisions is delegated up the line, whereas responsibility for definition and action remains always at the base, where authority for effort resides. "The formulation and definition of purpose is then a widely distributed function, only the more general part of which is executive" (p. 233).

DISTRIBUTION OF FUNCTIONS

With regard to distribution of functions, Barnard notes that executives may frequently find themselves doing nonexecutive work, and that sometimes this work is more valuable. The examples he cites are selling the product, settling some service complaint, or lecturing. He estimates that in an organization of moderate size, there may be 100 persons engaged part of the time in executive work, and some of these people are likely to be clerks or stenographers. "The work of cooperation is not a work of leadership, but of organization as a whole . . . Cooperation, not leadership, is the creative process" (p. 259). Barnard conveys the idea that executives have no separate concrete existence, but are parts or aspects of a process of organizations as a whole.

EXECUTIVE ABILITIES

Some of the general abilities needed by executives, according to Barnard, are general alertness, comprehensiveness of interest, flexibility, faculty of adjustment, poise, and courage (pp. 221-222). Specialized abilities can be acquired through training and education, "but we do not develop general executives well by specific efforts, and we know very little about how to do it. The higher the positions in the line of authority, the more general the abilities required" (p. 222). Barnard stressed loyalty as the single most important attribute or contribution required of the executive, adding that it is the least susceptible to tangible inducements (p. 220).

Thus Barnard the traditionalist makes the case that executives are important as catalysts and as coordinators, and they should be loyal and of good character and intelligent. Barnard the nontraditionalist argues convincingly that executive (or management) work is a cooperative effort in which all levels of the organization need to be involved, and that the creation of organization purpose, usually garnered by the traditionalist group as a special prerogative or duty of the manager, grows out of the aggregate actions of all and is a widely rather than narrowly distributed function. He also suggests that while one-tenth of the work in organizations may be performed by the management group, "at least nine-tenths of all organization activity is on the responsibility, the authority, and the specifications of those who make the last contributions, who apply personal energies to the final concrete objectives" (p. 232).

ORGANIZATIONS AND INDIVIDUALS

In his analysis of Barnard, Perrow (1972) contrasts him with Weber and other classicists along dimensions of control and the comparative rationality of organizations and individuals. Both Weber and Barnard believe that organizations are superior to (more rational than) individuals, but for different reasons. In the view of Weber and other classicists, the organization is a means of controlling individuals in the interests of the goals of its leaders. "The organization is more rational than the individuals because order is imposed upon members by those who control the organization, and the order is in the interests of goals or purposes established and guarded by those in charge." Whereas for Barnard, "The organization is more rational than the individuals because the organization is nonpersonal, or supra-individual; it is something that extracts from individual behavior the logic based upon common goals and willing cooperation" (Perrow, 1972, p. 81).

COOPERATION, NOT CONTROL

The absence of concern about control in Barnard's conceptualization is important. Since organizations are, by nature, cooperative, there is little need for control, and "the executive functions are to manage the system of cooperative efforts" (1938/1954, p. 216). In the previously discussed survey of public managers (Martin, 1981), top managers estimated spending about 34 percent of their time in controlling kinds of activities, and middle and lower levels of management estimated spending 43 percent of their time controlling. Assuming for the moment that there is some degree of comparability between private organizations discussed by Barnard and public organizations of today, these figures raise an interesting question: If we agree with Barnard that organizations are (or can be) essentially cooperative, requiring very little control, that public managers spend a great deal of time controlling, and that at least nine-tenths of organizational activity is performed by those who "apply personal energies to the final concrete objectives," how many fewer public managers than now exist at all levels would be needed?

Mary Parker Follett

The other proponent of cooperation whose views lead to similar questions is Mary Parker Follett. Like Barnard, she spent a great deal of time with managers and admired them; she conveys great optimism about the potentially positive effects of organizations on those within their boundaries as well as on society in general. Most of the selections in the book *Dynamic Administration* (1940) are addresses that she delivered to various groups over a number of years. (When quoting from these selections, the year given will be the year of the lecture or paper from which the quotation is taken.)

Like other writers cited in Chapter 1, Mary Parker Follett views management as generic. "For whatever problems we solve in business management may help towards the solution of world problems, since the principles of organization and administration which are discovered as best for business can be applied to government or international relations" (1933, p. 19). On an earlier occasion, she stressed that "the process of production is as important for the welfare of society as the product of production," and that the chief function and real service of business is "to give an opportunity for individual development through the better organization of human relationships" (1925, pp. 140-141).

COORDINATION AND COOPERATION

In a paper, "Individualism in a Planned Society," presented in 1932, she lists four fundamental principles of organization (p. 297), all focused on coordination:

(1) Coordination by direct contact of the responsible people concerned.
(2) Coordination in the early stages.
(3) Coordination as the reciprocal relating to all the factors in a situation.
(4) Coordination as a continuing process. "You have to have an organization which will permit an interweaving all along the line" [1926, p. 159].

Adherence to these principles would create an organizational climate different from that which exists in many organizations today. Mary Parker Follett believed that power and authority are overrated when identified with a particular person or group, and that power should be generated for all members of an organization, rather than divided, limited, or fought over. Her emphases on direct contact and reciprocity, and her insistence that a structure for coordination must be built in early rather than enforced toward the end of separate processes, remain in the mainstream of enlightened thinking today. Recurring themes in her work are: (1) interactive or reciprocal influence (power with, rather than power over), (2) circular behavior, (3) the law of the situation, and (4) functional unity.

Cooperation in observing the law of the situation is an important ingredient in her thinking about authority. It relates to her insistence that organizations are best when they are cooperative, unified entities, and that this vision of organizations makes notions of control less viable. "We shall always be seeking an external, and arbitrary authority until we learn to direct our efforts toward seeking the law of the situation" (1925, p. 112).

She reserves a special place for science and knowledge in creating better organizational worlds for people, and predicts that arbitrary authority will be diminished as more value is placed in the scientific method. She reinforces this by describing how knowledge has been used to discover the best ways of doing a job at the operating level and believes that orders are being replaced by "standard practices" (1928, pp. 273). Unlike Braverman, she extols the virtues of scientific management and what she sees as Taylor's contribution toward making job standards accessible to the workers. However, she adds that it would be entirely desirable to apply scientific methods to managerial jobs because managerial and administrative waste should be subjected to the same research as operating waste.

In very practical terms, Mary Parker Follett states that "the test of a foreman now is not how good he is at bossing, but how little bossing he has to do because of the training of his men and the organization of their work" (1928, p. 274). She believed that "the form of organization should be such as to allow or induce the continuous coordination of the experiences of men." Authority does not coordinate: "Legitimate authority flows from coordination, not coordination from authority" (1926, p. 150). "In the ideal organization, authority is always fresh, always being distilled anew" (1926, p. 151).

FUNCTIONAL UTILITY

Follett stresses that functional unity is the chief task of management, that the structure (organization chart) provides for this primarily, but that we look to the chief executive more than to any other person to make the organization chart a "going affair" (1927, p. 260). At another point, she speaks of the three functions of the chief executive as coordination, definition of purpose, and anticipation. "In business we are always passing from one significant moment to another significant moment, and the leader's task is pre-eminently to understand the *moment of passing*" (1927, p. 263). In her view, the leader (manager) releases energy and unites energies, and all with the object, not only of carrying out a purpose, but also of creating further and larger purposes.

DELEGATION

One issue that touches both authority and the functions of managers is that of delegation. Miss Follett deals with this perplexing management problem by observing that "the authority of the chief executive is not, in the best managed businesses, an arbitrary authority imposed from above, but the gathering up of many authorities found at different points in the organization" (1932, p. 296). She points out that the phase "delegating authority" assumes that the owner or chief executive has the "right" to all authority, but that it is useful to delegate some of it. Since authority goes with function, it is, and should be, widely spead throughout the organization.

FOLLETT VERSUS TRADITIONALISTS

The views of Mary Parker Follett are central to the development of a new set of assumptions guiding the proposed organization of work in public organizations to be described in the last two chapters. At this point, perhaps the best way to highlight the importance of her thinking is by comparing her views with traditional views on three major dimensions: the functions of managers, authority, and the manager's role in defining organizational purpose.

Functions of managers. Traditionalists tend to view management as an aggregate of planning, integrating, coordinating, and controlling functions, which are prerogatives of specified individuals called managers; Follett's view is that the necessary functions in organizations should be performed by those with the most knowledge, and such people may be found at any level of the organization.

Authority. A traditional view on authority is that managers should have the principal authority, and that specified amounts of it should be delegated "down the line" in proportion to the level of the person receiving it; Follett's view of authority is that it is the "gathering up" of many authorities at all levels of the organization, and that real authority is gained by cooperation in observing the "law of the situation."

Manager's role. Finally, traditionalists imply that the manager's role is to keep the organization together by providing it with purpose; Mary Parker Follett believed that managers should find and articulate the natural purposes and functional unity of the organization, recognizing that neither purpose nor unity can be imposed.

Summary

The major message from Barnard and Follett is that the successful accomplishment of organizational purpose requires cooperation rather than control. In preceding chapters it was argued that the functions of supervision and control are time-consuming activities for many public managers, often a personal "overlay" on existing bureaucratic control, and of questionable utility. Proposition 6 directs attention to the possibility of substituting the thinking of individuals like Barnard and Follett for the prevailing reliance on checking, directing, and controlling the work done in organizations.

Proposition 6: Cooperation, coordination, and obedience to the law of the situation can serve as alternatives to supervision and control.

Before bringing together the work of Follett, Barnard, and others to form a supportive theoretical network for an alternative approach to work in public organizations, two other subjects need to be explored. One is the success of various kinds of work redesign in the private sector, and the other is the discretion of public managers, to be addressed next.

CHAPTER 6

THE EROSION OF MANAGERIAL DISCRETION

> *As members of an organization rise through the hierarchy, they have increased degrees of discretion not to do anything at all.*
>
> —A. W. McEachern

The purpose of this chapter is to explore decision making at the upper and middle levels of public organizations, and to question the extent to which managers at these levels make critical decisions befitting their status and salaries. The proposition that will guide this discussion is as follows:

Proposition 7: Many managers at the upper and middle levels lack the discretion to make nonroutine decisions and are therefore unable to fulfill a traditional role expectation.

This proposition and others critical of the traditional aggrandizement of management are not intended to dispute the importance of some aspects of managerial work. A few imaginative individuals who rely on cooperation as the key process in achieving organizational objectives, and who are capable of coordinating decisions at all levels in an intelligent fashion, of attending to the external environment, and of giving expression to the broad goals of the organization, are needed in all organizations. However, there has been a tendency (discussed in Chapter 3) to *proliferate* highly salaried management positions throughout the upper and middle levels of public organizations. In evaluating that tendency, it is important to examine the reality in which most public managers operate.

Discretion at the Direct Service Level

Before focusing attention on managerial discretion at the upper levels, discretion at the level of direct service delivery should be briefly mentioned. Anyone who has worked in (or closely observed) organizations knows that some of the lower-level supervisory positions may be filled with what are called "working" supervisors; these are individuals who at times participate directly in processing the output of the organization. Frequently, they and the workers they supervise have considerable freedom to act in terms of selecting alternatives affecting the recipients of the organizational product or service, but have little discretion with regard to the policies and the internal procedures of the organization.

Police officers on the street, probation officers, nurses, social workers, and teachers, are among those whose wide discretion in dealing with clients, patients, students, or suspected criminals illustrates this point. Those who perform more routine but nonetheless important tasks also exercise considerable discretion in terms of the quality and quantity of their work. Examples include street repair and building maintenance personnel, gardeners, mechanics, and refuse collectors.

Without explicitly refuting the evidence about "doing" discretion, the trend continues to be one of emphasizing the appropriateness of salary and other distinctions between the activities associated with managing and those associated with doing. We are all so accustomed to the elevation of managers that it is difficult to imagine (let alone create) a public organization in which those who exercise a great deal of discretion at the service delivery or operating level of the organization, either professional or unskilled worker, receive the highest salaries.

The relative amount of discretion (used here to mean the freedom to act or judge on one's own), as well as the importance or complexity of such actions or judgments, is commonly used to distinguish upper-level from lower-level managers. Those lower in the hierarchy are usually expected to have less discretion than upper-level managers, and the decisions that fall within their more limited discretionary areas are perceived as less important, or at least more routine; stated another way, their decisions are more likely to concern the maintenance than the development of the organization.

Discretion at the Middle and Upper Levels

Challenging the expectation that upper and middle managers make important nonroutine decisions is the widespread phenomenon of perceived lack of discretion at the middle and upper levels of management in many of our public organizations. During a training program for middle managers from a department of human resources in a large east coast city (conducted in 1979), the single most frequently mentioned obstacle to the effectiveness of participants was, "We're told to manage, but we lack the discretion to do so." A related complaint was expressed two years later by middle managers from a large state agency, who felt they were spending most of their time combating or avoiding the unpredictable actions of their politically appointed top managers, and very little time making management decisions.

FEELINGS OF POWERLESSNESS

During a long-term consulting and training program with a department in a large county, discussions among the middle managers sometimes revolved around their feelings of powerlessness in making important decisions, and the powerlessness they perceived on the part of top administration who took their "orders" from the board of supervisors. (Doubtless conversations with board members would reveal their sense of powerlessness in the face of public demands and lack of resources. And to complete the circle, almost any citizen discussing government will eventually express his or her feelings of being powerless with regard to large bureaucracies.)

In one particular session, this group of county middle managers candidly discussed the dilemma of maintaining one's position and concomitant authority with those lower in the hierarchy, while at the same time experiencing powerlessness when it comes to bringing about needed improvements in the organization. Two of the reasons cited for the experience of powerlessness were: (1) the constraints imposed by the next higher level of authority (most of the participating managers did not have a "consultative" relationship with their boss, but merely carried out his or her directives); and (2) the proliferation of increasingly detailed rules and regulations governing almost all actions (the managers had not participated in the development of the existing policies and procedures and did not like many of them, but felt they had no power to change them).

FORMAL CONSTRAINTS

The regulations included both internal policy matters, such as those regarding the structure of the organization, the workflow, program and employee evaluation, and procedures for dealing with "problem" employees, as well as external matters such as new laws, or mandates from the board of supervisors. In their comprehensiveness, these formal policies and rules left the managers very little discretion and yet placed demands on their time and energy. Attempts were made first to understand and then interpret the formal policies to subordinates, who in turn "translated" them into action; since the rules were changed frequently, another demand was to keep "up to date."

Some of the existing problems perceived as *not* being within the purview of these highly paid managers in this particular department are widespread among public sector organizations: overly restrictive rules, lack of upward communication, a poor public image of the department, lack of reward for innovation, a declining budget and concomitant declines in the workforce and in the quality of service to the client, lack of support or recognition from "administration," poorly conceived procedures for handling layoffs and demotions, and a pervasive climate of distrust and low morale.

EFFECTS ON THE SUPERORDINATE/ SUBORDINATE RELATIONSHIP

The consensus was that things were getting worse in terms of discretion; these middle managers perceived themselves as having had more freedom to decide and to take action on more important issues in the past than they have now. They used the term "erosion" because the decline had been gradual rather than sudden. In discussing alternative ways of handling the uncomfortable erosion of discretion, a few of the middle managers said that they had adopted a strategy of simply recognizing what their subordinates could see for themselves: Managers in this department cannot make decisions on important issues. These honest acknowledgments of powerlessness apparently brought some degree of sympathy from subordinates, especially when the "boss" was faced with asking them to implement an unpopular policy from "above."

However, for many in the group, the overuse of "my hands are tied" explanations was perceived as risky, and they described themselves as aggressively asserting control whenever possible. They feared that a manager with an image of powerlessness could find his or her influence over subordinates faltering or failing to "work" the way it once did. For some of these managers, the tension surrounding this "balancing act," as one of them called it (feeling helpless and yet maintaining an authoritative image), was exacerbated by deeper feelings of uncertainty about their "worth" if they could influence neither policy *nor* subordinates.

The concern about their value to the organization was dramatized in a discussion about paperwork. Some of them felt burdened with the need to read and write many reports, and argued the advantages of keeping their office doors closed in order to accomplish these tasks. After listening quietly to this discussion, one manager remarked,

> We'll be cutting our own throats if we're unavailable [to the supervisors who report to us]; we can't do anything to change the administration, and the employees who report to the supervisors are the only people doing any real work. So if we set up obstacles that discourage subordinates from talking to us, we'll have no legitimate functions left.

Needless to say, not everyone in the room agreed about who is doing the "real work"; however, enthusiastic support for accomplishing work in an office with a "closed door" diminished sharply after that comment.

VIEWS OF A FORMER FEDERAL EXECUTIVE

The view from the top of a federal agency is significantly different from that described by the county middle managers, and yet it also conveys frustration at the lack of discretion. The former secretary of the treasury, W. Michael Blumenthal, observed that "in the government no one has the power to decide that this is the policy he wants to develop, these are the people who are going to develop it, this is how it's going to be decided, and these are the folks who are going to administer it" ("Candid

Reflections of a Businessman in Washington," 1979, p. 44). Blumenthal, who was the chief executive officer of Bendix before being appointed secretary of the treasury, related many of his comments to his perception that public officials generally have less discretion in terms of making their organization effective than do private managers. The activities associated with looking "good" politically seemed, in his view, to take precedence over being a good manager or a good administrator.

Mr. Blumenthal believes that those at the very top in government work harder, and with more frustrations, than their counterparts in business. He also deplores the "system" that keeps all those below GS 15 working less efficiently and more bureaucratically than *their* counterparts in private business due to what he calls an inverted pyramid in which "the amount of work varies with how far up you are—the people at the top do most of the work and have most of the pressure and cannot delegate" (p. 40). A major problem, as he sees it, is in the rank and file. Due to retirement policies and lack of discretion in hiring and firing, "some people just stay around and do little or nothing. So you see more and more people, a great many more than you really need" (p. 40).

One of several possible responses to these statements (and one that is particularly relevant to the problem of concern in this chapter) is to take issue with the inverted pyramid he describes and with the level at which "nonworking" employees are most likely to be found. The need for intelligent, hardworking executives has already been acknowledged, and the possibility of waste at any level cannot be denied. However, the proposition under consideration in this chapter is concerned with abuses at a different level: There are many highly paid positions that are considered part of management whose incumbents lack the discretion to make the important decisions their positions and salaries suggest, and who end up with "little or nothing" of significance to do.

Factors Influencing Managerial Discretion

SIZE, COMPLEXITY, AND INFORMATION OVERLOAD

A comment made frequently by managers when the subject arises of the need for comprehensive planning to improve organizational effectiveness is: "Unfortunately, all I do around here is put out fires." This lack of attention to the anticipation of problems and to planning their solutions, surely one of the most important functions of a manager, may be inherent in the growth of bureaucracies, and in the requirement to make policy decisions of enormous complexity. Ironically, the technological capacity to aggregate and even analyze information has not solved the basic problem, identified by some as the relative inability of any individual to comprehend the system when a bureaucracy grows to extreme levels of scale, complexity, and interdependence.

> The fact is that the stuff of public life seems to elude the grasp of many people. Bureaucratic processes have become specialized and professionalized. Yet, many of the larger bureaucracies are plagued with the unspoken but undeniable feeling among management and staff that no one truly is in control, that the dynamics of the organization are beyond the comprehension of any one individual.
>
> Nor does the mere aggregation of information necessarily contribute to the understanding of the system. Although the computer revolution has vastly increased the amount of information at our disposal, it has exacerbated the difficulty of decision-making by confronting the manager with a mountain of information that he has no hope of ever assimilating given the crisis management that prevails in many of the largest bureaucracies. Thus, the ability to collect massive amounts of information does not automatically assure that it will be used or be useful in the management of large systems. It is possible to be information-rich and knowledge-poor as a manager or consumer of public services [Elgin & Bushnell, 1977, p. 338].

CONTROLLING VERSUS MANAGING

In a thoughtful article about management, control, and decision making, Martin Landau and Russell Stout, Jr. (1979) describe their views of the unfortunate consequences of the popular phrase, "to manage is to control," They have a somewhat different view of the dangers of the computer revolution, arguing that in many public bureaucracies, there is a "vision" that Management Control Systems (MCS) are the answer to all organizational problems. These systems encourage what the authors call a Type II error, which is premature programming, or accepting as true a hypothesis that is false. Thus MCS are used to control a problem that should be managed.

One manifestation of the abuse of such systems is the forced routinization of problems. "In examining management curricula and practice, it is not unwarranted to conclude that all a good manager has to do is to learn a set of control procedures and to ensure that these are complied with. This is the way the routineer is made and he becomes, in Wildavsky's words, 'The problem he was designed to solve' " (p. 149).

The illusion that a complete control system is available may reduce the need felt by managers for the problem-solving and decision-making discretion some traditionalists have reserved for managers. Stated another way, MCS link discretion (the freedom to choose and act) exclusively with control, with the result that discretion is exercised not in the interest of experimentation and careful analysis of the results of policy decisions, but rather in the interests of searching for "deviants" among the subordinates involved in implementation.

PROTECTING AGAINST ERROR

Perhaps the most unfortunate consequence is that MCS reinforce attitudes toward error that have always prevailed in most large bureaucratic organizations. Too often, the effective performance of the organization goes unnoticed in the rush to retain power and control or to protect oneself from error.

Marked by *overdefinition* of rules and *overspecification* of tasks, Type II systems nurture the routineer.... Having learned that correct behavior is judged by conformity to rules regardless of result, he quite sensibly moves to avoid the exercise of discretion for such an act may easily be deemed an infraction. Given this perspective, subordinates faced with surprise demand even tighter rules in the interest of self-preservation. The system then turns in on itself [Landau & Stout, 1979, p. 153-154].

Thus conformity and the attempts to eliminate error become the consuming activities of managers and subordinates alike, even though it is apparent that compliance provides no information about outcomes and consequences, whereas errors are capable of informing. "In an intelligently managed organization, the information generated by anomaly, by discrepancy between expected and actual outcomes, becomes the means by which fallible rule sets are corrected and moved toward solution sets" (p. 153). The authors observe that, contrary to intelligent managing, "time after time, control systems, imposed in the name of error prevention, result only in the elimination of search procedures, the curtailment of the freedom to analyze, and a general inability to detect and correct error" (p. 155).

MODERATING EXPECTATIONS

Although the traditional literature providing an overview of management pays relatively little attention to the limitations of managers as they engage in the decision-making process, concepts such as bounded rationality, or "satisficing" (Simon, 1976), and of "muddling through" and "incrementalism" (Lindblom, 1959, 1968) have become popular and have tended to moderate expectations about what even the most excellent of managers can do. Other kinds of limitations, as noted above, are inherent in the size of bureaucracies and in the sheer quantity of information made available with computer technology (Elgin & Bushnell, 1977). Landau and Stout are critical of managers opting (with the aid of technology) for a mechanical kind of control, in lieu of managing. James Thompson adds yet another perspective by proposing that "when an individual believes that his cause/effect resources are inadequate to the uncertainty, he will seek to evade discretion." He explains that "when uncertainty looms large in comparison with predictive ability, judgment is suspended and other techniques, resorted to" (1967, p. 119).

Characterizations of Managerial Decision Making

Thus, in terms of decision-making discretion, a manager has been variously characterized as one who can do anything, one whose limited rationality causes him or her to make satisficing rather than optimal decisions, one who has been overtaken by organizational size, complexity, and information overload, one who allows complex decisions to be routinized and is reduced to seeking protection from error, and one who, under some circumstances, avoids exercising discretion. Another way of characterizing managers is to say that they, unlike many of their subordinates, have the discretion not to make a decision at all.

The limitations cited and presumed beyond the control of managers are difficult to argue with, and there is reason to forgive managers for their variable performance in making decisions. Organizations *are* getting larger and more complex, the information available *is* overwhelming, and there *are* human limitations in producing a flawless and comprehensive decision-making process. Somewhat less forgivable, but still understandable, are the actions taken by some managers who use their discretion in unnecessarily reducing decision making to a point at which it can be routinized and who avoid exercising discretion when it is not to their advantage to do so.

The important point is that these explanations, sympathetic of the plight of many managers, need to be examined in the light of other realities, particularly fiscal contraints. Consideration should be given to the cost of perpetuating or proliferating management positions where discretion, an important differentiating factor in terms of placement in the hierarchy and salary, is not exercised, regardless of the situation in which managers find themselves. Under these conditions (the nonuse of discretion), the high salaries paid to individuals occupying such positions become a legitimate public issue. (As one enterprising student asked during a classroom discussion of decision making, "If computers take care of routine decisions and lack of discretion or information overload makes nonroutine decisions impossible, are managers who make *no* decisions irrelevant to organizations?")

Data on Decisions and Discretion of Public Managers

REACTIVE DECISION PROCESSES

In one study of the decision-making processes of public managers (Clark & Shrode, 1979), the authors conducted extensive interviews with forty public sector executives in four state agencies and one federal office. The environments internal and external to a manager's position were identified first, and the decisions themselves were then analyzed.

> The manager's position was found to be ambiguously defined in an environment that tends to force reactive rather than reflective management. This finding stemmed from analysis of answers to questions dealing with the pressures the executives felt and the manner in which their duties were described. The most current pressures received attention without regard to their relative importance to overall long-term mission demands [pp. 344-345].

In terms of the actual decision-making process, findings in this study showed that these managers usually received messages or stimuli from the external or internal environment informing them that something about the organization was in a state of disequilibrium. "The problem was defined by the pressure perceived.... The manager's first reaction was to adapt to the pressure by developing alternatives that would lead to its rapid dissolution" (p. 348).

While the ability to develop alternatives is certainly part of the ordinary meaning of discretion, the hint that such freedom exists only or primarily under a kind of duress suggests more constraint than discretion. It certainly does not convey an image of a manager whose discretion allows him or her to plan, anticipate problems, and create a more effective organization. Apparently, the managers in the study reacted to those problems they experienced some pressure to solve, rather than giving attention to decisions that were important to the mission of the organization.

DISCRETION IN FORMULATING ORGANIZATIONAL GOALS

In another study (Martin, 1981), 183 public managers from a variety of public organizations were asked several questions relating to their discretion (freedom to act) with regard to hiring, firing, promoting, and improving efficiency. Also included were two more general or umbrella categories: improving organizational effectiveness and formulating purposes, objectives, and goals of the organization. The results for the 183 managers participating was an overall mean of 5.4 when all the activities were combined. (The scale used by respondents was from 1 = none to 9 = a great deal.) When the responses of 44 top managers were summarized separately, the overall mean discretion for the combined items was 6.8. Although this is a moderately high rating for perceived discretion, when asked "How much discretion do you have in formulating the purposes, objectives, and goals of the organization?" the mean rating (6.5) was next to the lowest (6.1 for firing).

These responses tend to confirm what is expected in distinguishing between upper and lower levels of management:

Those lower in the hierarchy, but still considered to be part of management, are more vulnerable to the erosion of management prerogatives than are top managers. However, it is also true that the next to the lowest amount of discretion was perceived by top managers in carrying out a function more descriptive of what an ideal manager does than any other single item on the questionnaire: formulating the purposes, objectives, and goals of the organization.

Summary

Many public managers complain that their hands are tied, that they lack the freedom to make important decisions. Among the explanations cited for this phenomenon are that managers frequently work in organizations in which formal rules take the place of many management decisions, that they (managers) are constrained by the levels above them, and that political maneuvering to stay alive in the system (or to deal with the sometimes unpredictable actions of a boss who happens to be a political appointee) has priority over creative efforts to improve the internal climate or service potential of the organization.

One study reveals that the perceived discretion of managers to formulate purpose, objectives, and goals is lower than for any other activity except firing employees. Another points up the fact that public managers make decisions in response to applied pressure from some source outside themselves; these are usually experienced as pressures to restore equilibrium rather than to develop or improve and therefore are likely to require remedies that are quickly translatable into routine maintenance activities.

Some have argued that by sheer size, complexity, and uncertainty in both the internal and external environments, bureaucracies are becoming unmanageable. Others have pointed out that the limited rationality of managers dictates satisficing rather than optimal decisions, and that various kinds of management control systems have promoted the tendency to routinize complex decisions, thus allowing both the manager and the managed to remain preoccupied with avoiding error.

One possible conclusion is simply that these and other conditions encourage public managers to refrain from risk taking and to become, at best, caretakers and maintainers; as long as the system remains as it is, little can be done to remedy the erosion of discretion in nonroutine decision making. Another conclusion (one more congruent with the preceding information and arguments) is that regardless of whether the amount of discretion to make important decisions is determined by managers' needs, fears, or preferences, or by organizational characteristics presumed to be outside their control, the salient question is whether or not they actually make those decisions necessary to carry out the functions justifying their higher status and salaries. If they do not (and while we're waiting for the entire system to be reformed), consideration should be given to reconceptualizing their role, and to reassessing the numbers of managers required in public organizations where this erosion of discretion occurs.

In preceding chapters, two terms were used to contrast the functions of managers: "developmental" activities, which are those associated with supplying purpose, coordination, resources, and protection to organizations, and "maintenance" activities, which are those associated with the more routine aspects of supervision, the maintenance of existing resources and procedures, and control. In the conventional view of management, both development and maintenance activities are needed. In order to develop the organization, the manager must control the work and the workers, and in large organizations, many layers of management will be required for full control. The information presented thus far suggests that this ideal combination is, at best, only half true. Maintenance activities are well taken care of and their importance reinforced when computers and MCS are utilized on their behalf, but developmental activities are all too frequently neglected. Thus we are confronting a myth, a gap between what managers actually do and what they are by tradition believed or expected to do.

If one accepts and wishes to act on the proposition that public managers lack discretion for developmental activities that, if performed, would set them and their salaries apart from others in the organization, one solution is to attempt to bring greater power to the position of manager in order to increase managers' discretion in carrying out the neglected activities; another is to improve existing (or create more) management control systems that tend to obscure the lack of developmental discretion by heavy emphasis on maintenance and control discretion. Both solutions are feasible without changing the traditional, hierarchical characteristics of bureaucracies. A third solution is that to the extent that managers lack or fail to exercise the discretion needed to make the important decisions for which they are presumably paid, their importance should be reassessed, and consideration should be given to reducing the number of managing or supervising positions.

As a step in that direction, attention will be given in the following chapter to how autonomous work groups in the private sector have challenged traditional management roles. Some of the ambiguous data about job satisfaction will be reviewed, as will the *Work in America* report, which encourages the redesign of work as a potentially successful strategy for improving productivity and the quality of working life. Work redesign and autonomous work groups have typically involved basic structural and role change in organizations, and they offer clues as to how to begin a fresh appraisal of work in public organizations.

CHAPTER 7

AUTONOMOUS WORK GROUPS

> *Simplified tasks for those who are not simple-minded, close supervision by those whose legitimacy rests only on a hierarchical structure, and jobs that have nothing but money to offer... are simply rejected.*
>
> —Work in America

Work redesign programs typically challenge the conventional "layering" of supervisory levels and the necessity of a sharp separation between managers and workers. They often include changes in existing work arrangements such as the creation of relatively whole, rather than fragmented, tasks, the introduction of autonomous or semi-autonomous work groups, and increased participation by workers in the decision-making process. The success of many of these programs has numerous implications, one of which is that some of the functions generally claimed as special prerogatives of management can be performed by workers.

Nontraditional Roles for Managers and Workers

TECHNOLOGY'S CHALLENGE TO SCIENTIFIC MANAGEMENT

In the process of searching for new organizational forms and new work processes to improve productivity and provide a better working environment, new roles for managers are created, and many of the old prescriptions for the manager/subordinate relationship are rejected. Eric Trist and others interested in the impact of technology on new organizational structures have pointed out that the worker in the second industrial revolution (one based on an information technology rather than on an energy technology) has a new role. The worker is a source of information for the management of technology, and so in fact is a part of management by becoming primarily fact finder, interpreter, diagnostician, judge, adjuster and change agent (Trist, 1970, p. 26).

The premises of scientific management described in previous chapters are antithetical to new work designs made necessary (or possible) by technological change. Scientific management encourages the notion that individuals and jobs have been "glued" together by supervisors, who in turn need supervisors, and so on, until the familiar layered hierarchy is achieved. The contention of Trist and others is that this "machine theory" of organizations has been overturned by science-based industries. "The autonomous work group . . . would appear to be the organizational paradigm which matches . . . the information technology. The advance of technology itself has reversed the world of Frederick Taylor" (Trist, 1970, p. 28).

A DIFFERENT VIEW OF TECHNOLOGY'S CHALLENGE

Braverman is one who has a different view of the impact of technology on the labor process. (He also would not agree that the world of Frederick Taylor has been reversed by technology; he believes that Taylor's influence is undiminished.) Using automatic data-processing systems as an example, he underscores the single-mindedness of capitalistic managers as they find ways of destroying a craft and ignoring the potential inherent in technology for greater autonomy and enriched jobs.

For a short time in the 1940s and early 1950s, the data-processing occupations displayed the characteristics of a craft. . . . The development of a data-processing craft was abortive, however, since along with the computer a new division of labor was introduced and the destruction of the craft greatly hastened. Each aspect of computer operations was graded to a different level of pay frozen into a hierarchy. . . . In early computer installations, the programmer was generally a systems analyst as well, and combined the two functions of devising and writing the system. But with the encroachment of the division of labor, these functions were increasingly separated as it became clear that a great deal of the work of programming was routine and could be delegated to cheaper employees [Braverman, 1974, pp. 329-330].

MANAGEMENT AS A PROCESS

Other organizational theorists hold views that are consistent with the basic premises of Trist's work. For example, McWhinney and Krone proposed a social system built around the idea of an industrial organization's "core process" or "product stream." One of their organizing concepts is that of semi-autonomous groups or teams. In this new configuration, "management is viewed more as a process than a role filled by a particular group of people" (McWhinney & Krone, 1972, p. 7).

It is not difficult to discern in this way of thinking a major challenge to the traditional views of management. To conceive of management as a process rather than as a role suggests, among other things, that the process might be handled by a wide variety of individuals at various levels rather than by a select group at the top. And the idea of semi-autonomous work groups is predictably unpalatable to those who believe that workers cannot function without the direction and control provided by a manager or supervisor.

In addition to opportunities offered (or neglected) by technological advances, three important forces have tended to push private organizations toward experimenting with autonomous or self-managing work groups. One of these is declining productivity resulting in lower-than-desired profit margins, another is the changing expectations of the workforce (and the high costs associated with a workforce in which absenteeism, sick leave abuse, and high turnover rates abound), and a third factor is the success of many experiments in various forms of self-management. The last two factors—changing expectations of the workforce and the successful experiments in work redesign—will be discussed in this chapter and the next.

Changing Expectations of the Workforce

JOB SATISFACTION

There is a prevailing popular notion that workers generally are not satisfied with their jobs, and yet survey results do not support it.

> The embarrassment with respect to job "satisfaction" measurement is that surveys of American employees continue to show that extremely high percentages of those measured report satisfaction with their jobs, while at the same time the incidence of decreased worker commitment as expressed through increases in absenteeism . . . , strikes (for other reasons than wages), employee rejection of negotiated contracts, and sabotage of product and plant is high and apparently becoming greater [Taylor, 1977, p. 243].

Reviewing a number of different studies that were conducted between 1954 and 1973, Taylor concludes that job satisfaction (or the absence of dissatisfaction) ranges from a low of about 79 percent to a high of 95 percent. These "good marks," however, need to be considered in the context of another phenomenon, which is that unidimensional questions such as "Do you like your job?" are likely to be viewed as meaningless (Do I like my job compared to what?) and yet may elicit a positive response. Katzell (1979) estimates that about 80 percent of the workforce describe themselves as satisfied with their jobs as a whole, and slightly over 10 percent express active dissatisfaction, but that only about 50 percent respond affirmatively when asked if they would continue in the same kind of work if they had a choice (p. 42).

High absenteeism and high turnover rates have plagued many organizations and appear likely to continue in the 1980s (Rosow & Zager, 1981, p. 19). If these are considered as behavioral indicators of dissatisfaction, how can the disparity between reports of relatively high satisfaction and the "dysfunctional" behaviors be explained? One possible explanation (in addition to the kinds of questions asked) is that questionnaires designed by social scientists, usually at a great distance from the workplace, may be treated with the same grudging tolerance as any form of outside meddling, that is, with suspicion or disdain, and with little effort on the part of the respondents to sort out or express their feelings or opinions. Still another plausible explanation is that individuals may wish to convince themselves as well as others that their job is satisfying (or at least that it has redeeming features), particularly if they have already invested many years in it and see little likelihood that they can find another job. To report general dissatisfaction, for some, would be equivalent to admitting their own inability or unwillingness either to change the existing work environment or to find something better.

Taylor recommends moving away from the use of simplistic measures of job satisfaction and argues for more specific indicators of how the quality of working life for given workers in given settings could be improved.

> Measurements should reveal the values of those being measured, should reinforce expectations regarding the ability to change, should provide a wide range of alternatives to present conditions, and should highlight dissonance between self and job to ensure a more human integration between them [Taylor, 1977, p. 249].

This recommendation clearly requires a situation-specific approach to determining job satisfaction. Braverman makes a similar point in claiming that only those who have been workers themselves or who "form their assessments from intimate contact and detailed information" can hope to understand workers' views and the complex conditions under which they work (1974, p. 30).

There is some evidence suggesting that satisfaction, however high in terms of the percentage of workers claiming it, has decreased. Surveys of approximately 175,000 employees in 159 companies covering a period from 1950 to 1978 show evidence of growing discontent. Size of the companies participating varies from 500 employees to more than 200,000. When the surveys were compared over time, the results showed a continuation of the familiar "hierarchy gap" (managers are more satisfied than clerical and hourly employees), and most employees think their company is not as good a place to work as it was in the past. "Discontent among hourly and clerical employees seems to be growing.... Both groups value and expect to get intrinsic satisfaction from work (e.g., respect, equity, and responsiveness) which were formerly reserved for managers" (Cooper, Morgan, Foley, & Kaplan, 1979, p. 118).

Quality of Working Life

Faced with signs of worker discontent and with declining productivity, professionals and academicians in both public and business administration have become increasingly interested in the overall climate of organizations, or what has been called *quality of working life*. An important and familiar question is whether there is a relationship between satisfaction with the quality of working life and worker productivity. The answer, equally familiar, seems to be: It all depends. Those who have sought to establish empirically a relationship between satisfaction and performance obtain mixed results, and there is no consistent evidence that good performance and high satisfaction are correlated. That is, both satisfied and dissatisfied workers may perform well or poorly. However, the lack of a definitive answer does not preclude the *probability* that in many organizations, improving the quality of working life will improve performance and raise productivity.

For some, improved quality of working life is a goal worth pursuing in its own right, regardless of any proven link with performance. However, it promises to remain an elusive goal since it is very clear that quality of working life is not an abiding, stable characteristic of organizations, but something that is always changing, depending on the needs, interests, talents, and expectations of the workforce. Some of the salient features of the quality of working life that have been identified are: adequate and fair compensation, safe and healthy working conditions, opportunities to use and develop the human capacities of workers, future opportunities, social integration in the work organization without prejudice, absence of stratification and a sense of community, interpersonal openness, privacy, free speech, equity, due process, and the opportunity to work in an organization that is socially responsive and relevant (Walton, 1974, p. 12).

Another important question is: Does a good, creative, or even adequate quality of working life prevail in most organizations today? Obviously, much depends on what is looked for as representing quality, and, of course, who is doing the looking. However, the consensus among those who study and write about organizations as well as among those known to this author who work in public bureaucracies is that it (high quality) does not prevail. "One need only go to work, read a newspaper, or talk with a neighbor to realize that problems of productivity and worker satisfaction abound in society. Poor-quality workmanship and productive inefficiency plague most sectors of our economy. Similarly, high rates of absenteeism, turnover, and counterproductive behavior are commonplace in both service and manufacturing industries" (Cummings & Molloy, 1977, p. 1).

Because it is so difficult for one person to determine for another what is and what is not "good" quality, an operational definition of quality of working life is that it is likely to be high or good when there is the opportunity for individuals to create for themselves the kind of work life they prefer. The vehicle that seems best suited to provide the maximum feasible opportunity for matching tasks with talents and preferences while still serving the major objectives of the organization is the semi-autonomous or self-managing work group, within which individuals may design their own jobs and work processes.

Work Redesign

CHOOSING AMONG TERMS

Before discussing the nature of such groups, it should be noted that the words *autonomous, self-managing,* and *semi-autonomous* are used fairly regularly together, and sometimes interchangeably. Autonomy is defined in the dictionary as "the condition or quality of being self-governing." When used within an organizational framework, the term "self-managing" can be viewed as almost synonymous with "autonomous." Those philosophically opposed to any encroachments on management prerogatives tend to favor softening or diluting the concept to the point at which it is in danger of extinction; when pressed, such individuals will favor use of the term "semi-autonomous." In order to reject firmly the views of those who fear *any* degree of formal autonomy for work groups and to support those who have a strong but realistic commitment to self-management, a better term might be *maximum feasible autonomy,* which carries the implication that a work group can achieve as much autonomy (independence or self-determination) as it desires as long as its autonomy is achieved within the context of situational requirements and organizational (as opposed to just management) objectives.

One of the assumptions in this study is that the nature of organizations requires that there must always be some degree of unity of goals, and that work groups, whatever they are called, must exist within that context. With this assumption clearly in mind, it becomes less important which term is used in general discussions. Obviously, the degree of autonomy and other characteristics of work groups must be made explicit during the planning and implementation stages of any work design program in which such groups are a component. Specificity of this kind is also essential to systematic research or the evaluation of work groups.

Generally, all three of the common terms—autonomous, semi-autonomous, and self-managing—will continue to be used, with a slight preference for the use of the latter term. One reason for this preference is that a major objective of this study is to promote the kinds of work structures that will lead, not to the elimination of management and supervisorial functions, but rather to their redistribution to work groups, reserving for top management discretion in facilitating internal cooperation and coordination, and in interactions with the external environment. As work groups absorb many of the functions previously assigned to managers and supervisors, they become increasingly "self-managing."

Many descriptions or definitions of autonomous or semi-autonomous work groups are couched in terms of the production settings that have been their "inspiration" and typical implementation sites. One definition that is general enough to cover many work settings is that "autonomous work groups are work structures where members regulate their behavior around relatively whole tasks" (Cummings & Molloy, 1977, p. 21).

Maxine Bucklow offers insight into the nature of the work group by comparing the thinking and the solutions offered by the human relations school growing out of the Hawthorne studies and the work done by Trist, Rice, and others in the Tavistock Institute. (She also uses a term, "responsible autonomy," which is congruent with the maximum feasible autonomy idea.)

> Responsible autonomy . . . gives the work group a central role in the production system, not the peripheral supporting role

envisaged by Mayo and Likert, and has successfully motivated rank and file workers to greater cooperative effort than other methods. It also makes more basic changes in the distribution of control and power, by transferring some of the traditional authority of management for the control and coordination of jobs, i.e., the part appropriate to the primary group's task, to the men who actually perform the task [Bucklow, 1966/1977, pp. 158-159].

A NEGATIVE ASSESSMENT

Not everyone agrees that autonomous work groups are either viable or desirable. Elliott Jaques, long associated with the Tavistock Institute, sees merit in the autonomous work groups of Emery, Trist, and others in the sense of providing freedom for groups and encouraging initiative. However, they are not, he insists, autonomous. "There is still an accountable manager who must oversee the work and judge whether the standards and methods are satisfactory, and if not, take steps to correct the situation" (Jaques, 1976, p. 272). In another section, he emphatically rejects the possibility that they can exist in bureaucratic hierarchies. "There can extantly be no autonomous work groups employed in bureaucratic hierarchies, regardless of the manifest description. There must extantly be an employed manager accountable for the work of the members of the group, and he must extantly assess each member's performance (pp. 201-202). He concludes that "autonomous work groups in bureaucracies are an organizational fantasy, giving the shadow of democracy without its substance" (p. 202).

WORK IN AMERICA: A POSITIVE ASSESSMENT

Perhaps the most popular and complete effort to document dissatisfaction and persuasively argue that the redesign of work is a desirable way to counteract it appears in *Work in America* (1973). "The main conclusion is that the very high personal and social costs of unsatisfying work should be avoided through the redesign of work" (p. 94). Some of the reforms and innovations designed for a General Foods manufacturing plant are cited as examples of how work redesign can improve the quality of work life. These include: (1) autonomous work groups, (2) integrated support functions (maintenance, quality control, and personnel functions are built into the operating teams' responsibilities), (3) challenging job assignment, (4) job mobility and rewards for learning, (5) facilitative leadership in lieu of "supervisors," and (6) self-government for the plant community (pp. 96-98).

The results of these innovations have been improved yields, less waste, avoidance of shutdowns, and a 40 percent smaller workforce than was anticipated during the planning stages. "Using standard principles, industrial engineers had indicated that 110 workers would be needed to man the plant. But when the team concept (rather than individual assignments) was applied, and when support activities were integrated into team responsibilities, the result was a manning level of less than 70 workers" (p. 98).

Other successful work redesign programs discussed in the report occurred at Banker's Trust Company, Traveler's Insurance, Corning Glass, Texas Instruments, and Motorola, Inc. In spite of numerous variations, all programs include worker participation in decision making, and many include some form of profit sharing. The kinds of decisions in which workers participate are those involving their own production methods, internal distribution of tasks, recruitment, and internal leadership, as well as decisions about what additional tasks to take on, and when to work (p. 103).

The report cautions that "not all of a company's decisions, of course, are turned over to the workers when they participate in management. Upper-level managers continue to run the company, handle major financial transactions, and coordinate all the functions" (p. 104). By contrast, the fate of middle and lower-level management is assessed less optimistically: In the redesign of work, some middle and lower-level management jobs are likely to be eliminated (p. 104). Later, in what could be called an understatement, the report points out that "certain problems are likely to develop when the traditional prerogatives of middle managers, as well as their jobs, are threatened" (p. 105).

The *Work in America* report was quite specific and generous in its praise of semi-autonomous work groups, making the point that the nature of the job itself is the key to quality of working life and that those actually doing the job should be instrumental in improving them. If one accepts as a working definition that quality of working life is high or good when there is maximum feasible opportunity for individuals to create for themselves the kind of work life they prefer, groups with "responsible autonomy" are logical solutions to poor quality of work life; such groups typically make decisions about how to improve working conditions and work processes so that they will better satisfy individual preferences within the constraints of the work team and organizational goals.

In addition to expanding areas of choice for individuals, work teams exercising responsible autonomy may contribute in another way to the improved attitudes and behavior verified by some of the experiments. That is, small self-managing teams offer more opportunities for close personal interactions than do the larger, administratively convenient departments typical of most bureaucracies, and they may be intrinsicially more satisfying for some individuals.

An appendix to the *Work in America* report contains abbreviated case studies of 34 organizations (or subunits) participating in what is labeled the "humanization of work." Ten of the organizations cited were in Holland, England, Norway, and Yugoslavia; the remainder were located in the United States. The problems that led to the innovations were, in almost all cases, those of low productivity, absenteeism, high turnover, and low morale. The solutions or the techniques used most frequently were those of expanding the freedom and responsibility of workers to set their own goals and standards and to make decisions related to their work. Terms frequently used to describe the techniques were: "less supervision" (in some cases, no supervision), "self-determination," "self-management," and "increased worker autonomy and responsibility."

The results claimed in these case study summaries were divided into "human" results, such as increased worker satisfaction, improved morale, greater job interest, and reduced number of grievances, and "economic" results, such as higher productivity, reduced absenteeism and tardiness, lower turnover rates, improved product quality, and less waste. Of those who specified the year in which the experiment was initiated, most (fourteen) began between 1966 and 1970, nine began between 1960 and 1965, three were (at that time) relatively recent (1970 or later), and two started their programs before 1960. Apart from any other success criteria, the duration of these work redesign programs is impressive.

Summary

Some of the background to work redesign has been presented in this chapter, along with a brief appraisal of the nature of autonomous or semi-autonomous work groups and the ambiguity surrounding job satisfaction and quality of working life. The *Work in America* report supports the proposition that increased autonomy for workers is not only a cost-reduction strategy, but that it also has the potential to improve the quality of working life.

In the next chapter, a number of additional studies will be cited in order to provide more recent illustrations of the work redesign (worker participation) experimentation occurring in both the private and public sectors.

CHAPTER 8

WORK EXPERIMENTS IN PRIVATE AND PUBLIC ORGANIZATIONS

> *Any organization, whatever its functions, goals, and environment, has to face change from within and from without.*
>
> —Michel Crozier

When he made the above statement, Crozier was in the process of an ambitious attempt to better understand bureaucratic systems by examining the ways in which they face change; one of the points he makes is that although a system may be extremely rigid and unable to correct its own errors (thus by his definition qualifying it as a bureaucratic system of organization), the rigidity can "obtain only within certain limits" (1964, p. 196), and adaptation to change, however slow, is inevitable. Experimentation with work redesign and various forms of employee participation may be considered as one of many ways in which organizations face change "from within" (such as changing expectations of the workforce and declining productivity) and changes "from without" (such as declining resources and the public's demand for more responsive and effective organizations).

Private Sector Experiments

Some work redesign or employee participation experiments have proven "too successful," and have been stopped. For example, at Polaroid, a worker participation project was given (as part of the experiment) a particularly difficult production deadline, one that few anticipated they could meet. They did meet it, but the "experiment was liquidated, not for efficiency reasons but because democracy got out of hand" (Edwards, 1979, p. 156). In this case, the success of workers designing and carrying out a difficult production task raised uncomfortable questions about the need for managers and supervisors in the plant. Rather than attempt to answer them, the successful experiment was discontinued.

Numerous reports of more durable programs to encourage worker participation or to create autonomous work groups have appeared in the *World of Work Report.* In a Volkswagen auto repair facility at Bolidenplan, Sweden, an equally split bonus based on productivity, plus the creation of four semi-autonomous repair teams, reduced turnover from 60 percent to 10 percent four years after the experiment was initiated, and gross profits rose by 27 percent in three years. The experiment eventually involved all fourteen shops operated by Volkswagen in the Stockholm area ("Organizational, Wage System Changes," 1978).

Results of a survey of 58 business organizations in the United States that have been experimenting with job enrichment showed economic improvements as well as increased job satisfaction. (Most of the programs reported tended to enlarge the responsibility of workers for planning, directing, and controlling their own work rather than merely providing additional or more varied activities.) The results of the survey showed an average improvement of 21 percent in production output for 50 of the 58 companies, 32 percent improvement in job satisfaction for 39 companies, and 32 percent reduction in absenteeism for 38 companies. Turnover was reduced by 18 percent in 47 organizations, and nearly half of the 58 organizations were able to reduce their workforces, resulting in average wage savings of $4,387 per month. These reductions were achieved by transfers, promotions, or normal attrition, rather than by layoff (Alber, 1978).

Since 1981, managers and union members at the Aliquippa Works of Jones & Laughlin Steel Corporation have been utilizing labor/management participation teams, with benefits reported by both parties. Some of the subjects the teams have considered are energy conservation, performance improvement programs, product quality, absenteeism, and overtime. The plant manager claims that morale has increased and absenteeism decreased, and that there is better communication between workers and managers resulting from the weekly team meetings; the union president states that the company is now sharing more important information with the steelworkers. In the establishment of the participation teams, a ground rule is that all planning and problem solving must be done jointly (Casner-Lotto, 1982a).

The details of another labor/management program at a Shell Canada Chemical Plant (heralded as a quality of work life program) suggest a more radical strategy than that embodied in the problem-solving teams at Jones & Laughlin and elsewhere. "Fulfilling nearly all the plant's functions (except those performed by a 14-man maintenance team) is an 18-member shift team with a pool of skills rather than fixed job descriptions and set positions. . . . The entire plant hierarchy is extremely flat, with only three levels: the shift teams and their coordinators, operations managers, and the plant superintendent" (Wallace, 1981, p. 11).

Butler Manufacturing Company in Story City, Iowa (one year old at the time the report was written), assembles grain dryers, and the Story City plant is organized into self-managing work teams. One employee says, "Basically, you are your own boss" ("Self-Managed Teams at Bulter," 1977, p. 124). Employees design or purchase new products and tools and talk with customers. (There are four "supervisors" who are called unit coordinators for 150 employees.) Achievements in 1977 included unexpectedly good levels of output, profitability (20 percent higher than projected), a change in the ratio of direct to indirect labor costs from 60:40 to 75:25, low absenteeism (0.8

to 1.4 percent compared to a traditional rate in factory employment of 4 to 5 percent), low turnover (10 to 12 percent compared to a U.S. production worker average in 1976 of 35.4 percent), and good materials usage. Characteristics of the plant include frequent job rotation, weekly team meetings with rotating leaders, monthly plantwide meetings about finances of the company, team hiring and firing, and selection of supervisors (coordinators) by the workers. As a result of the rotation system, most people have had enough experience after one year to build the whole grain dryer (3000 parts) by themselves.

A network of 82 industrial cooperatives in the Basque community of Mondragon employ and are owned by 14,000 workers ("Spanish Industrial Cooperatives," 1977). In 1976, collective sales were $336 million, up sevenfold in ten years. The cooperatives have a 3:1 ratio between highest and lowest paid, compared to 15:1 ratio prevailing in comparable firms. This means that "the lowest level workers in Mondragon cooperatives earn considerably more, and top executives considerably less, than their counterparts in private industry" (p. 129). At the end of each fiscal year, surplus is divided into three parts: 10 to 15 percent for community benefits, 15 to 20 percent to a reserve fund for the cooperatives, and 65 to 75 percent distributed to members in proportion to the number of hours worked during the year and to the respective rates of pay. In some firms (such as Copreci), assembly lines have been eliminated in favor of work tables "at which semi-autonomous teams organize their work and coordinate their efforts with other departments for the supply of raw materials, maintenance, and shipping" (p. 131).

RECENT TRENDS IN WORK REDESIGN

Quality Circles. Many of the recent reports of efforts to include workers in participating in organizational life, particularly problem solving, have focused on the successful utilization of quality circles. This is not as new a technique as is commonly believed; Honeywell is just one example of a firm that has had quality circles (QCs) since 1974 (Soyka, 1981). A report on the popularity of the QC concept (Plous, 1981) cites a few of the other companies that use quality circles: Hewlett-Packard, American Airlines, Harley Davidson, Intel, Metropolitan Life Insurance, General Electric, and Rockwell International. According to this report, no one knows for sure just how many businesses are experimenting with quality circles, but a consulting firm that trains facilitators to teach the technique estimates that there are about 400 American organizations using the basic concept.

A New Role for Labor Unions. In addition to increased emphasis on quality circles and flexible work schedules (the latter is discussed later in this chapter), two other trends should be noted; one has been identified as a "new direction for labor." Several significant unions (the United Auto Workers at General Motors, Ford, Chrysler, and American Motors plants, Communications Workers of America, the International Brotherhood of Electrical Workers, the Telecommunications International Union, and the United Steelworkers of America) are attempting to substitute cooperation for conflict in labor/management relations, to increase worker participation, and generally to improve the quality of working life (Rosow, 1982).

Employee Ownership of Firms. The second trend is toward employee ownership of firms. It was a rare phenomenon in the early 1970s, but it is estimated that there are now 5000 employee ownership plans, with between 2 and 3 million individuals involved. Although some problems with employee ownership are noted, the expansion in the number of such firms is attributed to the many successful experiences on record. One study reports that they are 1.5 times more profitable than comparable conventional firms ("Encouraging Employee Ownership," 1982).

As a specific illustration of the trend toward employee ownership, a story appearing in *Time* describes a situation in which employees of a failing hydraulic hose plant in Youngstown, Ohio, decide to buy the plant and run it. In December 1979, productivity was up 40 percent and profits of $600,000 were double the owners' initial projections. There was a reduction in the workforce (from 375 to 130 employees), longer hours, fewer benefits, lower salaries for top managers, and higher morale.

A CRITICAL VIEW OF WORK REDESIGN PROGRAMS

Although this chapter focuses on the success of work redesign, reports that are critical of these programs should not be overlooked entirely. Hackman (1975/1977) cites some of the failures in work redesign and finds the then existing research quite inconclusive in assessing the validity of the claims made either by advocates or by opponents. Among the causes he attributes to the inconclusive nature of the research is the way in which work redesign efforts are frequently reported ("more evangelical than thoughtful"), weak or incomplete methodologies in evaluating the effects of changes in work redesign, and the relative dearth of economic data such as direct and indirect costs and benefits (pp. 97-98). "In sum, it appears that despite the abundance of writing on the topic, there is little definite information about why work redesign is effective when it is, what goes wrong when it is not, and how the strategy can be altered to improve its general usefulness as an approach to personal and organizational change" (p. 98).

In succeeding portions of the selection cited, Hackman attempts to provide information relevant to these questions. He points out that although there is no universally good design, there are some specific factors to consider in order to achieve a successful redesign effort. These are: individual differences, interpersonal relationships, organizational climate and style, and technology (pp. 115-128). He also provides useful guidelines for installing planned changes in jobs: a diagnosis of the work system before a change is implemented, a focus on the work itself, advance preparation for unexpected problems, continuous evaluation, early confrontation of difficult problems, and the design of change processes to fit change objectives (pp. 148-158).

In spite of his reservations, Hackman conveys a degree of optimism about the benefits inherent in this group of strategies. He concludes by pointing out that work redesign is in its adolescence and must mature quickly if it is to survive and develop (p. 159). Judging by the examples cited in this chapter, work redesign has continued to be an influential change strategy in the intervening years since that material was written.

FLEXIBLE WORK SCHEDULING

One aspect of work redesign that promises to flourish during the 1980s is that of flexible work scheduling, which in effect allows workers to self-manage an important resource—their time. In *New Work Schedules for a Changing Society,* the authors state that the new and varied work scheduling programs "reflect the capacity and inventiveness of an open, democratic society that is ready to permit employees to take full responsibility for their attendance and performance at work without undue surveillance, controls, and restrictions" (Rosow & Zager, 1981, p. 4). The study forecasts that by 1990, "twenty-five percent of full-time nonagricultural workers in the United States will be on flexible work schedules, 5 percent will have compressed workweeks, and 28 percent will be engaged in part-time work, job sharing, and work sharing" (p. 4).

Another prediction is that by 1990, employers will recognize the economic and social advantages of new work schedules as a "fast-track method of meeting employee demands for better quality of working life" (p. 4), particularly when the employees themselves help plan and design the programs (p. 6). The greatest single obstacle to new work schedules, according to the report, is the "autocratic tradition of supervision" (p. 5). One of 50 recommendations contained in this study stresses the importance (when implementing flexitime) of ensuring a consensus among top managers in favor of increased choice and control for workers. "Productivity can be increased by letting workers sort out their own work schedules, and labor costs can be decreased by reducing the amount of supervision" (p. 60).

While it can be expected that flexible work schedules and other work redesign efforts will better meet the expectations of a "new breed" of Americans (Yankelovich, 1979), there are reasons to be cautious in predicting how far and how fast American organizations will move. Those that have embraced various forms and degrees of self-management clearly represent only a small fraction of the total number of organizations in this country. Some of the many factors to be weighed when considering work redesign are the technological requirements of any given organization, the status of its labor/management relations, the nature of the tasks performed, the competence of its work force, the resistance to be expected from groups and individuals within its boundaries, and the political and philosophical climate of the nation as a whole.

Rosow points out that although many of the success stories about increased democracy in the workplace emanate from the United Kingdom and Western European nations, states with relatively similar industrialization patterns and political democracy to that of the United States, the European trends are *not* a harbinger of the future in this country. He lists several factors that have fostered the progress of industrial democracy in Europe: higher rates of unionization, strong political affiliations of unions, the anticapitalistic philosophy of some union leaders, occupational and social immobility of the labor force, greater role of government in social policy, and centralization of collective bargaining (Rosow, 1979, pp. 176-177).

Public Sector Experiments

However one evaluates them or predicts their future, there is general agreement that programs involving greater worker participation, semi-autonomous work groups, or flexible work scheduling have occurred largely in the private sector. (Of the 34 case studies in the appendix of *Work in America,* only one, the Ohio Department of Highways, was a public organization.) However, a number of reports published more recently serve to illustrate work experimentation in the public sector. (The first five of the following seven examples were reported in *The World of Work Report,* published by the Work in America Institute.)

An experiment with quality circles at the Norfolk Naval Shipyard produced net savings of $150,000 in the first year after deducting all costs of operating the program. Productivity was up, an improvement attributed by a shop general foreman to the fact that the approach is based on a belief that "the resident experts are the people who do the work" (Law, 1981, p. 3). Their plan at the time the report was written was to increase the number of circles from 9 to 36.

Another quality circle pilot project occurred in Wake County, North Carolina, in which a total of 185 employees volunteered to participate. These individuals were organized into teams to meet on a regular basis for the purpose of identifying and analyzing problems; when this stage was completed, the teams made presentations to management about their findings and recommendations. Proposed projects were discussed in special workshops designed to provide training and support for the process. "In total, 39 quality circle teams identified improvement ideas worth approximately $151,000 in net first-year savings" ("Quality Circles Boost Productivity," 1981, p. 67). "The North Carolina project has successfully demonstrated that the QC approach to consensus management has a place in government offices as well as in private industry" (p. 68).

The City of San Francisco has been involved in a union-initiated Work Improvement Project since 1978 that is designed to improve the delivery of public services and to enhance the quality of working life for employees. Before participating in the project, managers and union representatives in each department sign an agreement that productivity gains are to be used to improve public service rather than to reduce employment. There are now labor/management work site committees operating in three different locations (the San Francisco Housing Authority, the Department of Public Works, and the City Commission on the Aging) representing about 2,000 of the 24,000 employees working for the city. Typically, these committees address problems of quality of supervision, job security, job stress, work procedures, and service delivery. Labor and management both continue to support the Work Improvement Project and new committees are being formed. Although the program is expanding, not all reactions are entirely positive; "Even in departments in which top management has committed itself to the program, the suspicions of lower-level managers still have to be allayed" (Olsen, 1982, p. 27).

Great improvements have been reported in New York City's Sanitation Department Bureau of Motor Equipment. "Changes have occurred gradually through a combination of carefully orchestrated teamwork, top-level managerial commitment and, most important, labor's involvement in issues affecting working conditions and productivity improvement" (Casner-Lotto, 1982b, p. 57). There are sixteen shop-level labor/management committees throughout the Bureau of Motor Equipment, which is responsible for the maintenance and repair of a fleet of 5000 trucks. Savings attributed to the new system have been estimated at more than $16 million. Shops are called "profit centers"; in each shop a "profit" is recorded if its output in terms of product or service costs less than if the transaction had occurred in the private sector. A 1981 report showed that the eight shops together had an annual net "profit" of more than $2 million. Another significant improvement is that 85 percent of the fleet is operating, compared with approximately 50 percent when the new director took charge in 1979, and the morale of workers is greatly improved. When discussing the inception of the program, a sentiment expressed by workers is that "for the first time, employees were involved in decisions that affected their work lives and, as a result, started to care about their jobs" (p. 61).

New York state has developed a number of programs, such as quality circles, employment continuity, job training, and on-site day care, all designed to improve the quality of working life of state employees. These programs have developed through the joint cooperation of the Office of Employee Relations and the state's major union. "Together, they have developed one of the most extensive quality-of-working-life agendas in the public sector" (Casner-Lotto, 1982c, p. 65).

In 1976, when Santa Clara County in California faced a deficit, the management proposed a reduction in both work hours and pay for all employees. Countering through their unions, employees requested a voluntary work-sharing program. This resulted in a plan (which went into effect even though the deficit did not materialize) under which each employee may request a reduction of work time and pay of either 2.5, 5, 10, or 20 percent for six months at a time. Although the numbers of those volunteering had declined from 15 percent of the workforce in 1976 to 4.5 percent in 1979, part-time work and job sharing (encouraged in the same agreement that allowed the flexible work time and pay reductions) showed a steady increase during this period (Rosow & Zager, 1981, pp. 120-122).

A three-year, nationwide voluntary experiment on alternative work schedules has been underway in the federal government, in which more than 250,000 federal employees in about 1,100 work units are participating. The program started in 1979, and schedules being used in the experiment include flexitour, gliding, variable day, variable week, maxiflex, and compressed schedules (GAO, 1980). In each of the models, employees are granted some degree of increased discretion in the amounts and intervals of time they spend at work, provided they work a prescribed number of hours or days in a given period of time.

The GAO report was concerned mainly with presenting evidence to support its contention that the Office of Personnel Management has used sampling procedures and methods of analysis that will not yield the data Congress needs to evaluate the success of the program. However, the fact that the experiment occurred at all can be interpreted as a sign that the federal government, along with the city, state, and county examples cited earlier, is attempting to experiment with new ways of adapting to a workforce with changing needs, attitudes, and expectations.

Summary

The purpose of presenting examples of some of the work experiments conducted within both public and private organizations was in part to make the point that organizations can indeed adapt to change, often creatively. Another related purpose was to develop a more receptive mood in which to consider the alternative approach to work arrangements that will be described in some detail in the final chapter.

The battle for improved organizations is far from being won. Work experiments of the kind described are still the exception rather than the rule for business (and there are significantly fewer such experiments in the public than in the private sector). Also, as was pointed out, not all such programs have shown good (or at least desired) results (Hackman, 1975/1977; Edwards, 1979); indeed, some of the "successful" programs described here may have since failed. Nevertheless, as reports of either successful or unsuccessful work redesign efforts circulate in the environment, they provide information, stimulation, and guidance to those in organizations who are facing change and seeking ways of adapting.

One impression derived from this review of case studies is the great variety in the programs described; categorization and labeling, if desired, would be difficult since each program has unique features that differentiate it from others. Perhaps a suitable general term (in addition to work experiments) is that used by *Work in America* in an appendix, "Case Studies in the Humanization of Work" (p. 188). There is, however, one distinction of importance for this study: Some of the programs involve little or no change in the basic structure or the formal roles of members within the organization, while others require such changes. For convenience, the former can be identified generally as employee participation strategies, and the latter as work redesign strategies.

A characteristic of work redesign strategies is that they usually include changes such as increased autonomy and responsibilities for work groups organized around relatively whole tasks; many of these programs have altered the basic structure of organizations and have challenged the traditional prerogatives of supervisors and managers. While it is true that employee participation strategies may have the advantage of posing relatively little threat to established groups, they may also fail to make the more basic and lasting changes that are needed in many organizations.

Whatever the strategy selected, the spirit of innovativeness discernible in these case studies brings a degree of cautious optimism concerning a proposal (developed in ensuing chapters) to reduce the numbers or functions of supervisors and managers and to create self-managing enclaves in public organizations. The caution is warranted by the fact that the approach clearly represents a step beyond flexible work schedules, employee participation, and quality circles; the optimism is warranted by the great variety of successful programs presented in this chapter. A tentative conclusion is that the proposal is in less danger of being dismissed out of hand than it would be if, for example, no evidence existed to support the concept of self-management. This conclusion is the basis for Proposition 8.

124 MANAGING WITHOUT MANAGERS

Proposition 8: The successes of work redesign encourage continuing experimentation with new approaches that utilize self-managing concepts.

The next tasks are to examine some of the current problems faced by government that exacerbate the need for innovation, to summarize all the propositions, to formulate the central recommendation growing out of this study, and to discuss the myth of management.

CHAPTER 9

THE MYTH OF MANAGEMENT

> *They go to the office in the morning, make a cup of tea, read Reference News, have a chat with someone and read any documents that come along. Sometimes they hold a meeting on something or other, say a few things that don't really matter. Then the day is over.*
>
> —From an editorial about government bureaucracy in China appearing in the *People's Daily* and reported in the *Los Angeles Times,* February 2, 1982.

Many signs point to a need for a full range of experiments to improve the image and effectiveness of government agencies in the United States. Although our government workers may be less vulnerable to criticism of the kind being levied in China as that nation reportedly undertakes various reforms to reduce the numbers of bureaucrats by one-third, popular sentiments in this country continue to run cool when it comes to government. Expressed demands from the public to keep down the costs of government are certainly not new, but the success of recent forms of "taxpayers' revolts" have transformed these familiar demands into concrete action.

Cutbacks in Government

PUBLIC SENTIMENT IN CALIFORNIA

In a *Los Angeles Times* poll, 66 percent of 1473 adults contacted in California were still strongly supportive of Proposition 13, passed in 1978. Most (65 percent), wanted even deeper cuts, particularly in government employee wages, but generally did not want cuts in services such as libraries, garbage collecting, public transportation, highways, schools, hospitals, and parks. About 70 percent of those polled (Democrats, Republicans, and Independents) said there is "still a lot of fat" in government (Endicott, 1981, p. 1.).

TRENDS IN DEALING WITH DECLINING RESOURCES

While the New Federalism as projected involves a steady transfer of programs and taxing discretion to the state governments over the next few years, it is apparent that the resources to support government at any level are in short supply; many predict a worsening of the government's fiscal crises. At all levels of government, program reductions (or elimination), budget cuts, layoffs, compulsory furloughs, promotion freezes, or demotions are occurring or being considered.

In attempting to meet the challenge of declining resources, local governments are contemplating some dramatic changes during the next twenty years. Predicted trends include consolidation of cities, consolidation of services, various joint powers agreements, contracting for services from private firms, differentiated service levels, coproduction (groups can contribute private resources in the delivery of public services), direct cash grants to needy individuals, increased use of fees as revenue (permits and licenses), increases in user charges, assessment districts for neighborhoods that desire (and pay for) a particular public service, and creation of municipally owned banks, with profits going to the general fund (Mars, 1980-1981, pp. 24-33).

These current and predicted changes relating to government bureaucracies and how they function are examples of the numerous plans, proposals, and creative ideas being circulated in an effort to deal with a changing philosophy about government, as well as with the actual shortages and cutbacks. However, there are few if any suggestions directed toward new work arrangements that would reduce the numbers and functions of the managers and supervisors employed in the vast government workforce. This may be due in part to the efficacy of the myth that organizations cannot function without a special group called managers.

Review of Propositions

The propositions presented and elaborated in previous chapters form a foundation on which to explore the myth of management and to build an alternative approach to the organization of work responsibilities in some public bureaucracies:

(1) The belief that managers are supremely important to organizations has dominated the literature (Chapter 1).
(2) Managers more frequently engage in routine maintenance kinds of functions than they do in conceptualizing problems and opportunities or in planning for the development of the organization (Chapter 2).
(3) The managing/doing dichotomy, or the separation of conception from execution, serves to keep the labor process dependent on management, thus ensuring the continued importance of a group of people called managers (Chapter 3).
(4) Average grade escalation and narrow spans of control intensify the need for experimenting with alternatives to the managing/doing dichotomy (Chapter 3).
(5) After an initial period of orientation and training, most individuals can perform their work without supervision (Chapter 4).

(6) Cooperation, coordination, and obedience to the law of the situation can serve as alternatives to supervision and control (Chapter 5).
(7) Many middle and upper-level managers lack the discretion to make nonroutine decisions and are therefore unable to fulfill a traditional role expectation (Chapter 6).
(8) The successes of work redesign encourage continuing experimentation with new approaches that utilize self-managing concepts (Chapter 8).

The Central Proposition and Underlying Assumptions

The ninth and final proposition is central to the presentation in Chapter 11 of a new approach to work in some of our public bureaucracies:

> **Proposition 9:** A reduction in the numbers and functions of superordinates and the creation of self-managing work groups would respond to pressures to reduce costs and at the same time provide an opportunity to improve the working environment and performance of government employees.

The general assumptions on which this recommendation is based have been developed in the preceding propositions, but there are three specific assumptions underlying it that bear restating:

(1) After an initial orientation or training period, the actual human labor applied in the creation of the central product or service (doing) does not need to be directed or controlled by others (managing or supervising).
(2) "Doing" activities are the most important of all organizational activities.
(3) Those who do the work are in the best possible position to decide on the division of responsibilities, the work standards, and the work methods.

The Nature of The Myth of Management

A major obstacle to any serious consideration of the ninth proposition is what may be called the "myth of management." In Chapter 1, the management aggrandizing tendencies in the literature were described. Illustrations of how the literary heritage of managers is seldom realized in actual work settings, thus creating a "gap" between expectations and performance, are presented in subsequent chapters. A myth is defined in the *American Heritage Dictionary* as "one of the fictions or half-truths forming part of the ideology of a society; a notion based more on tradition or convenience than on fact."

The ideology surrounding management in our society is that only managers can and should perform the important functions deemed necessary for the survival and success of organizations, and further, that in order for the organization to be effective, they must direct, control, monitor, and discipline others. (This is commonly expressed as "getting the work done through others.") The evidence that is available suggests that this is a convenient half-truth, thus qualifying it as a myth: While real managers, especially those not at the top of the organization, lack the time, ability, discretion, or all three for the developmental functions that are presumed critical to survival and success, they do invest tremendous energy in maintaining the organization by directing and controlling others who actually do the work of the organization.

DURABILITY OF THE MYTH

One of the possible reasons why the myth is so durable and active is that its basic assumptions are rarely made explicit. Three important assumptions believed to underly the myth are:

(1) The actual human labor applied in the creation of a product or service must be controlled by others not directly involved in the labor.

(2) Those who labor directly on this product or service are (and should be) paid less than those who control or manage them.
(3) Without this control, the work would not get done and organizations would fail.

The myth is strengthened by the fact that in many organizations, managers become symbols of order and stability, regardless of any specific functions they perform. Furthermore, managers occupy positions and claim salaries that others aspire to, and these aspirations, in combination with the symbolism, are seen as part of the "glue" that holds the organization together. As long as these values prevail, and as long as the above assumptions remain unquestioned, they act to guard against, or successfully block, any alternatives that challenge them.

Traditional Strategies versus New Work Arrangements

Evidence presented earlier suggests that managers themselves would prefer to be more productive and creative—more involved with development and less with routine maintenance, control, and handling occasional crises—but that they lack the discretion to do so. This lack of discretion, some would argue, is the real enemy: We don't want fewer managers; just give them more discretion by fighting the "system" that keeps their hands tied. Others supplement this approach by calling for more training that will give managers the skills and confidence to become more proactive in finding or creating the discretion they need. Others argue that managers will only utilize discretion when it is in their best interest to do so, from which one might deduce that situations need to be created in which managers will find it feasible (safe and profitable) to exercise discretion. These argument have merit, but there are few signs that the strategies they suggest have been successful in correcting this problem; indeed, managers complain more and more about their lack of discretion in bringing about significant improvements in their organizations.

The approach recommended by the proposition under consideration is to create new work arrangements. Excessive layering and the managing/doing dichotomy are important obstacles to organizational effectiveness just as intergovernmental mazes, ambiguous laws, and unnecessarily rigid controls from legislative bodies may be obstacles to the full utilization of managerial discretion.

Ideally, all such obstacles should be examined and reduced wherever possible. However, the distress in which government at all levels finds itself requires careful attention to the potential viability of the various strategies. Role changes of the kind mandated by the propositions in this study seem more likely to lower costs and improve performance than, for example, training efforts to bring superhuman skills and attitudes to existing managers, or efforts to wrest more discretion for managers from city councils, boards of supervisors, state legislatures, or Congress. Solutions to the problem of poor communication and coordination among judicial, legislative, and executive branches of government, as well as among the various levels of government, promise to come to fruition very slowly. In the meantime, costs are high, the public disaffection with government is high, and remedies to deal with organizations *in situ* are badly needed.

Beneficiaries of the Myth

The myth of management is so well established that it is difficult to gainsay. When things are going well with an organization, it must be that it is well managed; when things are not going well, it must be that the organization needs more or better-trained managers. It is easy to speculate about who benefits from the perpetuation of the myth; managers, management educators, trainers, and consultants come immediately to mind. There is also evidence (Chapter 4) that nonmanagers have mixed feelings about managers and supervisors, and that in fact many of them my contribute toward keeping the myth alive. Their support may be variously interpreted as a need for order, security, assurances of "equitable" treatment, a buffer, or an incentive in the form of promotions to higher-paying management jobs. Many subordinates sense (or have been taught) that they are dependent on managers for their security; although such dependency could, over time, be unlearned, it cannot be denied that without the myth, there would be fewer managers and inevitable reductions in the prospects for promotion.

The Promotional Opportunity Dilemma

The expected resistance to lack of promotional opportunities does, however, need to be examined in the light of existing circumstances. For many public organizations, there is already a freeze on hiring, raises, and promotions, and for the U.S. workforce as a whole, the demographic composition has shifted to the point at which there is an excess of middle-aged people poised for promotion who will inevitably be disappointed. It is predicted that by 1990, there will be 60.5 million workers in that age group, compared to 39 million in 1975. This represents a dramatic 55 percent increase. The "middle-age bulge," as it is sometimes called, suggests that there will be intense competition for promotion "coupled with substantial career disappointment for many and the possibility that persons in the 25-44 cohort of 1990, some of whom have already entered the job market and already suffered from being born in a large group, will receive especially low relative income for their entire lives" (Freeman, 1979, p. 75).

This prediction suggests that, even if hierarchies continue undisturbed, there will be difficult times ahead for many employees interested in promotion; the situation is aggravated for public employees by recurring budget crises. Therefore, it is conceivable that an alternative work arrangement in which there are reduced numbers and levels of managers or supervisors will be considered by ambitious employees the lesser of two evils. Although the approach proposed contributes to an already serious dearth of opportunities for high salaries and for status as it is commonly construed, it also offers certain benefits, such as a new climate of cooperation, more challenging work, and more opportunities to use a wide range of personal abilities.

The largest group likely to acknowledge that it has something to lose by the myth and something to gain by the proposition is made up of members of the public at large. Their preoccupation with the growth and costs of government forecasts some degree of interest in strategies to reduce the numbers of positions labeled as "managers" or "supervisors." Their support would increase if they had reason to believe having fewer such positions would release more individuals to perform functions that have a high priority with the public, thereby allowing reduced costs of government to coexist with improved quality of public service.

Summary

The propositions discussed in previous chapters and reviewed here have laid the foundation for consideration of the myth of management and for a recommendation to alter the approach to work in such a way that self-managing work groups will absorb many of the functions formerly reserved for managers and supervisors. This alteration will lower costs and provide an opportunity to improve the working environment as well as the performance of government employees.

Next, concepts addressed in previous chapters will be reviewed and combined in order to put the finishing touches on the case for self-management in public bureaucracies.

CHAPTER 10

COUNTERACTING THE MYTH

Before bringing together themes from various sources in opposition to the myth of management and in support of a self-managing approach to work in some of our public organizations, an opposing view will be discussed. It was selected because it deals with broad concepts concerning life in modern bureaucracies in a unique way, and because it suggests why a nonhierarchical approach should *not* be considered. It also highlights the concern for accountability, which many believe is an important dimension of organizational health threatened by the advent of autonomous or self-managing groups.

Stratification and Time-Span Analysis

In his book, *A General Theory of Bureaucracy* (1976), Elliott Jaques expresses the belief that stratification is permanent, universal, natural, and desirable; in bureaucracies, persons can be stratified following a time-span analysis. The "maximum time span within which a person is required to act with respect to all of his tasks in a bureaucratic role does appear to give a measure of the level of his work" (pp. 107-108). If bureaucracies would continue to follow their natural inclination to stratify, but do so on a work capacity basis, Jaques apparently believes it would be possible to create "more requisite institutions to replace the pathological ones" (p. 376).

In more operational terms, stratification would solve pay and promotion problems because pay is automatically experienced as fair if one is in the proper stratum based on work capacity, and promotions would be based on capabilities and readiness for a longer time span and a higher stratum. It would also, for many bureaucracies, reduce the numbers of levels to those necessary for the scope of work desired by the organization. Jaques's research apparently reveals six or seven levels that correspond with a consistent and definable depth structure, one that appears to be "universal and constitutes one of the fundamental properties of bureaucratic hierarchies" (p. 127). Within this structure, Jaques sees that equality of opportunity for progress is necessary to enable everyone to maintain a C-W-P (work capacity, level of work, and pay) equilibrium.

Human capability as a criterion for promotion has more to recommend it (and is more difficult to measure) than the criteria utilized in some organizations, such as gender, friendship, or age, and it is more sensible than seniority alone. However, the time-span rationale preserves hierarchy, and it corresponds with the notion, deeply ingrained in most organizations, that long-range planning and projects are reserved for, or assigned to, those in more highly paid positions. It is interesting to speculate what the answer might be if, instead of asking employees (who are familiar with the traditional values and procedures for determining rates of pay) about the "fairness" of their own pay, they were asked about the "worth" of functions independent of given positions. For example, if they were asked, "Is it more important to fix the pothole in the street (short time span) or to put the finishing touches on a bus transportation plan for consideration by the City Council (long time span)?" the answer might well be, "Both are important and 'worth' about the same amount."

The point is that it is highly debatable whether time span of functions form any more of a "natural" hierarchy than do the more conventional (though less desirable) rationales, or whether, as Braverman and others might contend, the isolation of such functions as long-range planning and their identification as being the exclusive domain of the highest-level positions was a deliberate, thoughtful process to ensure control of the "troops." From that perspective, it is only sensible, as organizations grow, to define each level descending from the top as having positions requiring less planning, fewer important kinds of decisions, reduced access to overall knowledge of the labor process and other information important to the survival or improvement of the organization, and of course, a lower wage. The way in which job descriptions are written is a clear demonstration of how these values have been perpetuated; as people enter organizations, they have a tendency to accept this gradation and to reflect that acceptance when judging the fairness of their own pay.

In spite of these reservations, the time-span technique for determining the number of levels required and the positions to be assigned to each level, and for making promotions, may indeed remedy many organizational ills. Reducing the number of levels by any means is laudatory. It is possible to view this technique not as a radical reform, but as an effort to deal sensibly with existing bureaucracies by providing them with an improved and more intelligent rationale for deciding the shape and size of their hierarchy, and for their placement and promotional policies.

However, Jaques's support of the superordinate/subordinate relationship and of bureaucratic hierarchies as potentially healthy and natural forms stands essentially in opposition to the propositions advanced in this study. While his ultimate goal, expressed as "the attainment of requisitely humanitarian systems... essential... for human progress in industrial societies" (pp. 376-377), is surely one that everyone can embrace, his assumption that large-scale institutions cannot prosper or even survive without someone (a manager) being accountable for the work of someone else (a subordinate) sounds very much like part of the conventional wisdom on management. Many writers and managers attribute great importance to accountability, and this concept is worth examining more closely.

Accountability

In a list of key terms in a book on organization behavior, accountability is described as "a person's obligation to carry out responsibilities and be accountable for decisions and activities" (Ivancevich et al., 1977, p. 560). Benveniste (1977) identifies three kinds of interventions associated with accountability. The first is to verify that monies or other resources are used for the purposes authorized (to minimize errors and corruption); the second is an internal process whereby an organization plans, budgets, schedules, implements, and evaluates its own activities; and the third is an external intervention to find out if the organization is doing what it is supposed to do (p. 141).

Although all aspects of accountability as defined are interrelated, attention at this point will be limited to the general and reciprocal accountability and responsibility of superordinates and subordinates. As Jaques expressed it, "Bureaucracies are work systems in which people are responsible for using their judgment and discretion in carrying out tasks on behalf of a manager who is accountable for their work" (1976, p. 62). This focus is not intended to minimize the importance of the overall performance of our public organizations, that is, the extent to which they do what they are expected to do with a minimum of waste and an absence of corruption. However, internal accountability is of particular concern in the development of new work processes and new role relationships, and thus will surely be of concern to organizations considering reductions in supervisory positions or experiments with any form of self-management.

Internal efforts to "tighten" or ensure accountability in most bureaucracies can do little more than reinforce existing features;

hierarchy itself is an accountability system held together by the "chain of command." Whether accountability is conceived as an addition to, or a reinforcement of, existing procedures, it is important to distinguish between the positive preventive attributes of accountability and the often negative consequences that follow its enforcement.

Most managers tend to describe accountability with the admonition that *without* it, "things fall between the cracks." If all the important tasks are not specifically assigned, and if someone is not "accountable" for these tasks, and if that someone is not carefully supervised, there will be "breakdowns" in the flow of work. At a more formal level of explanation, most people seem to agree that accountability programs have the potential to diminish error by encouraging analyses of the various steps in a work process so that it can become better understood. Also, they can serve to clarify duties and expectations; in conventional organizations, job requirements and supervisorial expectations need to be clearly stated, and few organizations clarify these as frequently as they might.

On the other hand, negative features typically described by those involved in an accountability "drive" are that such programs offer nothing more than excuses for managers to engage in blaming others with more impunity than they usually enjoy. Campaigns to eradicate error and inefficiency and to promote accountability often are invoked when things are not going well, and cynics have been known to accuse managers of inventing such schemes to divert potential criticism from themselves.

Errors, omissions, delays, and misunderstandings are present in any social system, regardless of its management philosophy, its structure, its workforce, or any other organizational characteristic. When considering the attractiveness of *preventing* or reducing errors or delay through an emphasis on accountability, that appeal should be weighed against the quality of relationships and the overall effectiveness of the organization that prevail *after* the inevitable errors or poor performance occur.

An example (a composite of many experiences) may serve to illustrate this point by tracing the events surrounding an error that occurred in a hypothetical, but not unusual, organization in which accountability is fully realized.

An Example

The management of this large public agency prides itself on making it clear to all employees the exact duties for which each is responsible, and in the case of supervisors, the exact extent to which he or she is accountable for the work of subordinates. Various records and reports are required periodically to emphasize the commitment of management to efficiency, the elimination of error, and to "tight" accountability. However, errors do not disappear in the wake of rhetoric or report writing and during an otherwise quiet month, an unfortunate event occurs: Erroneous data are discovered just as an important program is about to be launched; the error threatens to undermine the program because of the delay caused while new data are acquired.

At this point, management congratulates itself on discovering the mistake in time (a delay, though unfortunate, was preferable to the long-range consequences of the faulty data), and on quickly tracing it to its "source"; they attribute this efficiency to the organization's well-defined tasks and its emphasis on accountability. It soon becomes apparent that the error and subsequent delay has affected progress on other related parts of the program, including the work being done by an organization (X) at another (higher) level of government. For the purposes of tracing the drama that occurred after the discovery of error, let's assume that Supervisor B heads the erring unit, and that he is supervised by Manager A.

Manager C from afflicted organization X soon finds out that B's people are responsible for the error and the delay, but that B is accountable, and that A is accountable for B's failure. Tracing the exact amount of blame "due" each party takes considerable energy, but appears to be satisfying work. In a subtle way, B implicates his subordinates (whom he inherited from a previous lousy supervisor), B is formally reprimanded, and a host of conversations and memo writing ensue among the key actors, a group that has now grown to include A's boss, who dutifully reprimands A as the person accountable for B's poor performance.

When things go wrong in any agency, especially one in which error avoidance is a primary objective, each layer of accountability finds it relatively easy (in this complex and imperfect world) to implicate several other parties or factors in and out of their own organization. Eventually (as happened in the example) the event fades from the awareness of everyone concerned, but resentment and suspicion are very likely to linger and to grow. Cautiousness will spread and innovativeness decline. B's performance may or may not improve, but unless he thrives on crises, he will be a little more cautious and at least learn how better to cover his or his subordinates' mistakes or lapses. (Shortly after the series of events described, he was heard to remark, "I guess I'll have to keep a tighter rein on my people.")

Except for the speed with which the failure is traced (and this may be important in some cases), positive benefits sufficient to compensate for the negative environment created when the search for a "culprit" is underway are difficult to identify. Perhaps more important, it is difficult to justify the enormous investment of time and energy required on the part of such a large number of individuals when the search for error (and for the person who committed it) is handled with the fervor often present when efforts to achieve "total accountability" are in full swing.

If one imagines a citizen standing at a counter, expressing a complaint about a service error and attempting to hold someone in this same large organization "accountable," the drama intensifies. If the complaint is accepted, the chances of that citizen tracing the person "responsible" are low, partly because it is very easy in a bureaucracy (with or without special emphasis on accountability) to disclaim knowledge of, let alone responsibility for, the error in question: "I took care of the paperwork on that promptly, and sent it to Section E." After a week or so of inquiry, Section E will respond that they never received the document, and so on. The skill and creativity with which many bureaucracies can deflect, deny, remove, or simply absorb complaints about error is truly impressive.

On balance, accountability systems that are internally initiated and implemented are most often utilized in the interest of preventing errors or delays, and, once the inevitable errors occur, allowing superordinates to fix blame on subordinates; accountability systems are most frequently ignored when challenged from the outside, particularly if the challenge comes from a source perceived as powerless. To emphasize this point, a student in a course on bureaucracy described a typical reaction of employees in a regional federal agency office when a client wishes to see the "manager" in order to lodge a complaint. The person receiving the request will go to the most "officially" attired of his or her colleagues on this particular day, who will in turn play the part of the manager to placate the client; in most cases, the "acting" manager will "dead-end" the complaint, particularly if it involves any extra work or if it reflects poorly on any of the conspirators. These actions are perfectly understandable in an organizational environment in which employees can avoid punishment or even be rewarded when they deny (rather than learn from) error.

The approach being recommended in this study takes a different view of accountability; it is based on the belief that deemphasizing (and in some cases eliminating) the conventional manager/subordinate relationship will have a largely salubrious effect on many public organizations. The approach visualizes work groups in which individuals are more responsible and accountable to their goals or purposes, and to what Mary Parker Follett would call the "law of the situation" than they are to their bosses. A climate will be created in which employees see more benefit in examining errors in order to improve the work processes than in tracking down and blaming those who committed them. Many of those now tied up with telling others what to do and in being accountable to and for others, will be "free" to deal directly with the products or services of the organization and with the public who use them.

Four Themes Reviewed

Four major themes developed earlier form a foundation on which to build a case for self-management as a viable structure in some public organizations. The themes will be reviewed briefly and synthesized in support of the proposition that a reduction in the numbers and functions of superordinates (who in many cases are performing unnecessary functions) and experimentation with various forms of self-management will lower the cost and improve the effectiveness of many public organizations. Some of the essential functions now being performed (or neglected) by a multitude of managers can be performed by a few top managers, while other essential supervisory functions can be performed by subordinates. In the next chapter, a practical application of this approach will be described.

MANAGERIAL DISCRETION

The first theme is related to managerial discretion. If it is true that public managers have available to them a great deal of discretion in determining the performance of public bureaucracies, then perhaps we should, as most people assert, have better, not fewer, managers and find other ways of saving money. However, there is evidence suggesting that managers do not have sufficient discretion to warrant their high salaries. Impersonal "governance" by formal and comprehensive rules and regulations in many public sector bureaucracies have reduced many managers and supervisors to offering redundant control.

When faced with a wide variety of decisions regarding personnel administration, the budget, new or deleted programs or functions, or work standards, the public manager (especially if he or she is not a top manager) can honestly say, "It is out of my hands." When dealing with matters such as personnel policies, even top managers in some departments (such as those in counties with large and influential central personnel components, or in a multitude of state and federal agencies) perceive that such decisions are beyond their range of influence; they resign themselves to merely implementing the rules, and to submitting any conflicts about the rules "back to personnel." Many of the historic gains in public administration that have sought to impose uniform rules and regulations for all government employees can be viewed as challenges to the necessity of managers and supervisors, some of whom draw large salaries to act as an interpreter or defender of rules handed down to them.

Some admit that routine decisions have been usurped, but claim that managers are still proactive in making broad policy kinds of decisions and are clearly leaders in the sense of forging new directions for their agencies or departments. Countering this assertion is evidence that managers perceive and exercise relatively little discretion at the level of organizational change and improvement, or goal setting (Martin, 1981), they suffer from lack of time for leadership and for long-range planning (Lau et al., 1980), their decisions are made primarily in reaction to outside pressures to restore equilibrium (Clark & Shrode, 1979), they are busy routinizing work so that it can be controlled by MCS rather than managed (Landau & Stout, 1979), and they suffer from information overload, which hinders rather than helps their decision-making processes (Elgin & Bushnell, 1977).

All of which runs counter to the popular idea that the job of top managers has a large conceptual component or requires an abundance of conceptual skill (Katz, 1955/1974; Hersey & Blanchard, 1977). If many managers do not (for whatever reason) have the discretion to change the nature and direction of their organization, to make long-range plans for the future, or to introduce improved personnel practices to their workers, the question that arises is how many fewer managers than now exist are needed in our public organizations?

HUMAN RELATIONS AND JOINING MEANS TO ENDS

The second theme is concerned with the "human relations" component of a manager's job, judged by Katz (1955/1974) to be essential to effective administration at every level. Hersey and Blanchard also identify human skill as the "common denominator that appears to be crucial at all levels" (1977, pp. 6-7). In a sense, human relations can be thought of as "rescuing" public managers from the oblivion of dissipated discretion with regard to broad policy issues or with regard to the more routine but nonetheless important decisions usurped by rule proliferation and computerization. To the extent that the important goals and objectives of an organization are determined by law (or by directives from a central administration to which managers and others have no access), and to the extent that the implementing procedures are determined by formal rules and processed automatically, a manager or supervisor is surely in danger of becoming obsolete unless he or she can utilize human relations skills in dealing with subordinates.

Thus, one way of obviating the danger of obsolescence is to give attention to activities that have rarely been challenged in the past as legitimate prerogatives of managers: personalized supervision and subordinate development. If this focus is combined with the belief that these activities as practiced are of great value and require nonroutine decisions, the conclusion is one that neatly turns the threat of computers, for example, into an asset while at the same time enhancing the importance of managers. "Management development will take a more prominent place in future organizations. . . . As computers take over routine decision making, tomorrow's manager will have more time to devote to unprogrammed activities such as solving human relations problems and developing subordinates" (Bass & Ryterband, 1973/1974, p. 400).

There has always been considerable controversy surrounding the human relations movement or "school" as it is sometimes called. Those promoting attention to human relations believe that consideration of human needs and capacities is indispensable to organizational effectiveness, and that it is necessary to be aware of how people individually and in groups think, feel, and behave at work. They typically urge managers to study and attempt to understand human behavior; implicit in their message is a request that managers themselves behave sensitively and "humanistically" in their dealings with employees.

For some, human relations literature and training has been tainted by a parental "being nice to employees" flavor, or by a "learning to understand human behavior so that we can better predict and therefore control subordinates" undertone. At its best, of course, one can interpret the major theme as being that of assisting those in organizations to realize their full potential while at the same time improving organizational effectiveness. Unfortunately, the results of several decades of experience with human relations programs, even for ardent proponents, are often disappointing; in spite of some successes, disgruntled, misbehaving, and "unactualized" employees continue to proliferate in the halls and offices of both private and public organizations.

Unfriendly critics believe that much of what passes for human relations is nothing more than the means of "adjusting" workers to the principles of scientific management (Braverman, 1974), unnecessary meddling with the ideas or attitudes of employees, or that it is a "plot" on the part of the vested interests in the organization to quiet the potential trouble makers and to make palatable what is essentially disagreeable in organizational life. In discussing the role of psychologists in the field of organization theory, Alberto Guerreiro Ramos warns that too often practitioners and consultants subscribe to an ideology aimed at integrating the individual and the organization. "Relations between individuals and organizations always imply tension and can never be 'integrated' without crippling psychic costs" (Ramos, 1981, p. 70).

In spite of these criticisms, the emphasis on human relations continues in many organizations, albeit in new guises and under new labels. Managers or supervisors in large public bureaucracies who enroll in (or are sent to) courses in human relations are often skeptical that positive changes in the organization are possible. However, many still seek to ease some of their personal pain and disillusionment and find such courses helpful in doing that. Others may have secret misgivings about their worth to the organization; they may consider translating and enforcing rules that someone else makes, scheduling and assigning duties to subordinates, or attending long meetings that have negligible output, as insufficient justification for their positions or salaries. Learning how to be good at human relations may assuage some of those misgivings.

Many years ago, Selznick distinguished between leadership and administrative management, by suggesting that the latter deals with the implementation of goals that are settled, (the joining of "available means to known ends"), whereas the leader is involved in choices that affect the basic character of the enterprise (Selznick, 1957). The point of concern over 25 years later is that there are fewer and fewer such choices, but more and more managers with increasingly settled goals, and that the basic task of joining means to ends has to some extent been simplified by automatic data-processing systems. The shortage of meaningful functions appears to have been mitigated in part by urging managers at all levels to acquire more sophisticated interpersonal skills, to be more concerned about how they treat subordinates. What makes this advice problematic is that even when these skills have been well learned and implemented, the margin of improvement in the quality of working life is disappointingly slim.

It must be acknowledged that managers and supervisors who still struggle with the complexities found in joining available means to known ends face difficult tasks, often made more difficult than need be by forces totally out of the control of those individuals. Also, they can (and usually do) make a qualitative "difference" by influencing *how* the organizational goals will be achieved, and even how the mandated policies will be passed on to the "troops."

What is disputed is that these functions and the decisions involved should be reserved for a special group called managers or supervisors. The abilities to join means with ends, and to decide how best to implement policies and when, how, and by whom the various tasks will be performed are important, but not rare. Individuals working directly on processing the output of goods or services more than likely possess those abilities. If, as proposed, employees are organized to work in small groups in which these functions could be distributed and matched with workers possessing the most suitable skills and interests, organizational costs would be lower, and, because of the increased autonomy and challenge to those doing the work, organizational performance could be expected to be higher. The troops can be governed *directly* by the goals and rules of the organization, and by the "law of the situation."

Under existing structures, there is a tendency for middle managers and supervisors to grow accustomed to passing along directives from "above"; they may complain about administration to consultants and to each other, but rarely do they become active in joining forces with others at their level to *influence* top administration. Except for the occasional maverick, incumbents of the middle positions in the hierarchy tend to be docile and well mannered in their dealings with those "above" them, preferring not to "rock the boat."

If these positions were eliminated in favor of self-managing teams, one can only speculate about the teams' relationship with top management or with central administration. There is certainly no reason to believe that they would be any more docile than individuals in the chain of command, many of whom learned to "play the game" of accepting their orders from above soon after their arrival on the organizational scene. In the course of acquiring self-managing skills and some degree of unity, self-managing work groups could (eventually) be expected to become more proactive than individual supervisors in modifying ill-conceived policies from the "top." (One difficulty with these speculations is that, except in cases in which some form of self-management was imposed on an existing organization, only in reasonably flexible organizations could one except to find experimentation of this kind, which suggests an administration already more willing than most to modify policies and procedures.)

DECLINING ORGANIZATIONS

A third theme is related to the special nature of government organizations in this country, now, and in the forseeable future. Many are classified as declining organizations; the fiscal crises, public disenchantment with government, and the decreasing numbers of employees and agencies at the federal, state, and local levels have already been cited. Caplow (1976) points out some of the difficulties in the management of declining organizations, one of which is the low morale of employees. He warns that the difficulty grows if there are multiple problems that the organization cannot solve through any effort of its own. His recommendations for declining organizations include the reduction of administrative overhead at a rate faster than that utilized for other activities and the elimination of the nonessential, while saving or reinvesting in the essential functions of the organization (pp. 183-185).

In the process of eliminating the contrived differences between managing and doing, a great deal of personal time and energy would be released for the "essential functions" of the organization. Whether this additional labor comes from administrative or staff positions or from unneeded supervisors and managers, the desired result is the same: the elimination of the nonessential and the promotion of the essential functions of the organization.

THE SUPERORDINATE/SUBORDINATE RELATIONSHIP

The fourth and final theme is that of the interpersonal content of the superordinate/subordinate relationship, and the necessity of supervision. Since the bulk of most managers' and supervisors' time is spent in an activity called supervision, the necessity of that function becomes critical to any consideration of changes in the work they perform. While many managers, when asked, consider supervision to be important as well as time consuming, many nonmanagers, when asked, say they can perform their work largely without supervision. However, most nonmanagers take a dim view of the effect of no supervision and especially of no supervisor on their own satisfaction, on the effectiveness of their work unit, and on the satisfaction of others in the unit (Martin, 1981).

Settling the issue of how much supervision is necessary to organizational effectiveness will require more empirical evidence than is now available. Even with additional research, no single answer will suffice, but it may be possible to develop better procedures by which each organization can measure its own need for supervision. In the meantime, a tentative conclusion reached earlier is that public organizations can no longer afford to attend to the conflicting desires and ambivalent feelings surrounding supervision if by so doing they avoid experimenting with the potentially cost-reducing configurations that would require far fewer supervisors than now exist.

Those who work in organizations or are organization watchers can attest to the dominating influence, for better, or for worse, of the superordinate-to-subordinate relationship on the overall organizational climate. Observations of life inside hierarchical organizations lead to some tentative conclusions about the creativity or productivity *drain* inherent in the activities that characterize that relationship. Subordinates are engrossed with pleasing, second guessing, getting even with, subverting, protecting against, or merely avoiding the boss. Such activities can (and often do) exhaust workers to the point at which they are less able to perform the tasks for which they were presumably hired. Certainly, there is much less time in which to perform them.

Superordinates, on the other hand, are engrossed in controlling the behavior of, motivating, rewarding or punishing, looking good to, or being fair with subordinates. Such activities, however well intentioned, either actively divert superordinates from exercising whatever discretion they have in developing the organization or provide an added excuse ("I'm attending to human relations") for not doing so. In either case, it is an expensive and time-consuming set of activities.

Summary

Several messages can be discerned in these various supporting themes that counteract the messages in the myth of management. In many public organizations, the "glue" ostensibly supplied by management is already provided by well-defined rules, rights, and policies. Attention to improved interactions with employees may or may not be harmful, but is very likely unnecessary, and the "games" generated endlessly around the superordinate/subordinate relationship constitute a serious time and energy drain. Declining organizations should, more then others, concentrate on the essential functions. And finally, the discretion of managers about important matters is sufficiently low that serious questions arise as to the utility of some management positions. In spite of all this, organizations today continue to cut primarily from the bottom, protecting the bulge of middle managers and the status quo of an elite group at the top.

Some readers may agree that there are unnecessary management and supervisory positions, but disagree about what should be done about it. In considering the proposal that (1) the numbers of management and supervisory positions should be reduced whenever possible, and (2) self-managing groups should be established, it is quite possible to agree with the first point and to disagree with the second. Both steps are recommended in this study because of the belief that self-management strategies represent a positive force in their own right, that in time they will improve the quality of working life as well as the performance of public employees, and that their existence increases the feasibility of eliminating unnecessary positions.

It is recognized that reductions in management positions can be achieved through means other than self-management, as, for example, in eliminating an entire level of supervision, not filling vacant management positions, and adopting a policy requiring wider spans of control. (Such actions will probably require other actions, such as redesigning the flow of work, adjusting pay scales, dealing with the resistance to the changes, or training people to handle wider spans.) But whatever the adjustments selected or required, it is hoped that those who believe there is an oversupply of managers and supervisors in a particular organization but who are not sold on self-management will not be distracted from inventing their own unique strategy for accomplishing a reduction in these positions.

The possibility of experimenting with work redesign and self-management in public agencies is enhanced by evidence suggesting that most employees can perform their work without ongoing supervision. Mary Parker Follett's wise admonition to follow the law of the situation deserves fresh consideration in any new organizational configuration that will reduce the numbers of supervisors and increase the numbers of individuals engaged in the essential functions of the organization. If, as she believed, cooperation and coordination under this law are the essence of organizational health, additional people (including those "released" from managing and supervising) involved cooperatively in performing public services should bring renewed vitality to the internal climate of public organizations.

CHAPTER 11

AN ALTERNATIVE APPROACH TO WORK AND RELATIONSHIPS IN PUBLIC ORGANIZATIONS

Based on the arguments presented in the preceding chapters, an alternative to the traditional definition of work responsibilities can now be examined within the context of existing organizations. One fairly detailed example will be given, and another presented in summary form.

Self-management is a convenient umbrella under which to discuss this particular alternative approach to work, but it has the disadvantages of association with a philosophy that may predispose some otherwise open-minded public administrators to dismiss the idea out of hand. A term that may more accurately reflect the assumptions underlying the approach is "goal-directed work groups." However, regardless of what it is called, the alternative to be presented is intended to encourage other adaptations congenial with the spirit in which it is offered: Since many employees in public organizations can plan their own work and determine how to do it within the general context of agreed-to goals, unnecessary levels of supervision should be identified and eliminated.

Example 1: A Parks and Recreation Division

The example selected is a parks division of a municipality located in Southern California. The division was selected on the following criteria: (1) It is small enough to permit description. (2) It is a line department performing functions that are common to most if not all city and county governments. (3) Some of the functions require specialized knowledge but generally they are familiar and largely routine, which permits either lay or professional judgment as to the feasibility of the approach. (4) It is relatively streamlined in terms of its existing ratio of manager to nonmanager (that is, it is not top-heavy), and from informal interviews, it appears to have an enlightened, interested, and relatively young management. The fourth criterion is important. It is relatively easy to propose changes and anticipate improvement in an "unhealthy" organization; to do so in one that is essentially "healthy" increases the probability that a large number of organizations may benefit from the approach described.

As shown in Figure 11.1, the top management position is that of director of parks and recreation; the incumbent reports to the city manager. This individual is responsible for two divisions, Parks and Recreation, but only the former will be analyzed. The Parks Division is organized into four units, three of which represent geographical areas in the city and each of which has a "hierarchy" identical with the one shown for Section 1 in the figure. The fourth unit is for park building repair and maintenance only.

The equipment operator's position is shown according to salary, that is, between gardener 1 and gardener 2, but the position description specifies that the incumbent will, under supervision, perform semiskilled work of a mechanical nature in the operation of automotive and maintenance equipment, but will not supervise anyone. Thus the position is shown apart from the chain of command.

The building repair section has a foreman, six building repairmen, and four maintenance men. Although each of the park sections has its own maintenance men, none has a building repairman. The latter are dispatched as needed by the building

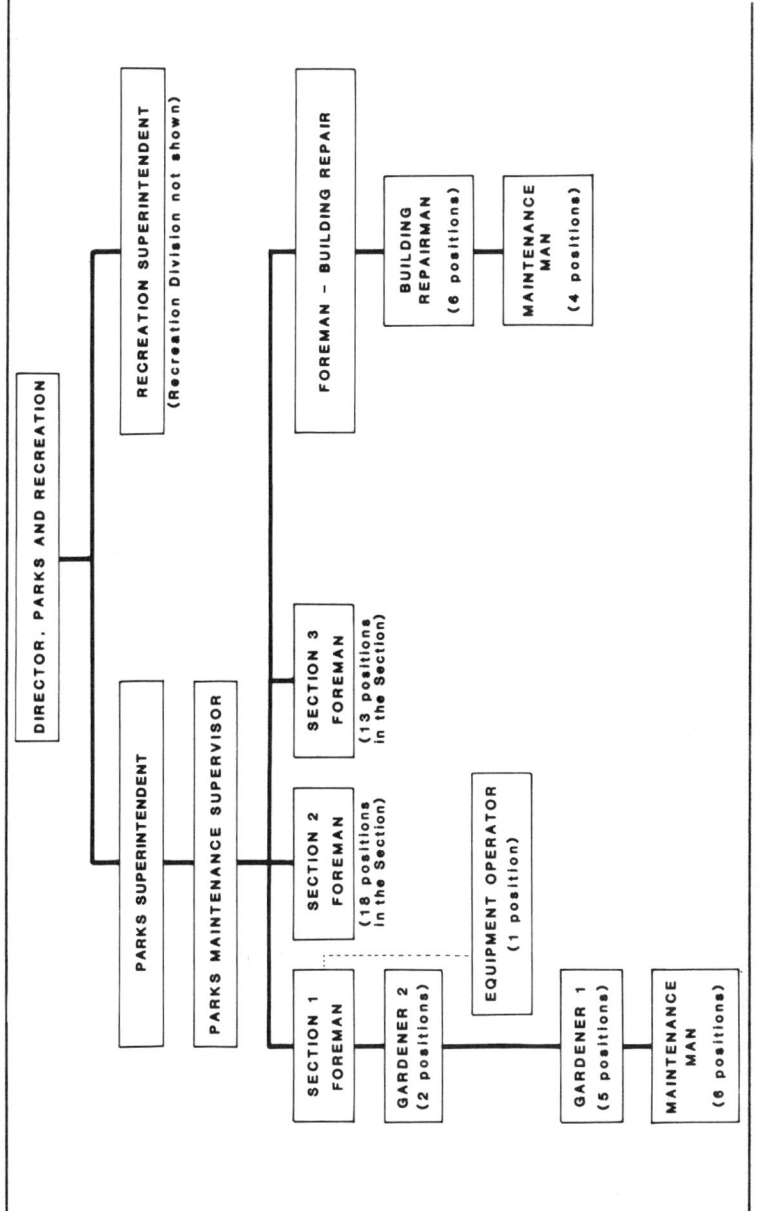

Figure 11.1: Partial Organization Chart of a Municipal Parks Division

155

repair foreman to any one of the parks in the three geographically located sections, as are additional maintenance men on an as-needed basis. The entire division includes sixty persons, one of whom (the director) is top management, two of whom are middle management, and four of whom are first-line supervisors or foremen. (Excluding the foremen, this is a modest ratio of approximately one manager or supervisor for every nineteen workers; including foremen, it is a still reasonable 1 to 7.5 ratio.)

The purpose of the division is clearly stated as developing and maintaining public parks and recreation areas, allowing for maximum use of leisure hours in aesthetically pleasing and safe surroundings. The job descriptions for each position class are informative, and are summarized below.

Maintenance man: Under close supervision performs routine unskilled manual work in the maintenance and construction of parks, streets, and utility systems. Examples of work: digs holes for power distribution, backfills and floods trenches, assists in planting and irrigating, erects bleachers and stands, sweeps, cleans, operates small power tools.

Gardener 1: Under direct supervision performs routine, semiskilled maintenance work involving the care of parks and areas around public buildings and facilities. Examples of work: mows, waters, edges, cultivates, plants and transplants, cleans, operates light power equipment, performs custodial work in community buildings.

Gardener 2: Under general supervision performs responsible and supervisory work in the cultivating, planting, and maintenance of landscaped areas of the parks, parkways, and around the various public buildings and facilities. Examples of work: acts as leadman in preparation, planting, and maintenance of lawns, shrubs, flowers, and ground cover; maintains and installs sprinkler systems. The remaining five activities listed begin with the word "supervises" followed by the functions assigned to Gardener 1 above.

Park foreman: Under general supervision, supervises and directs unskilled, semiskilled, and skilled workers in the construction and maintenance of parks and recreation areas. Examples of work: supervises all the functions mentioned above, as well as plans work, assigns specific duties to the workers, checks on their progress, trains employees, inspects equipment and tools, requisitions material.

Parks maintenance supervisor: Under general direction of the park superintendent organizes, supervises, and coordinates citywide maintenance and construction activities of the Parks Division. Examples of work: plans, supervises, and coordinates the maintenance activities and the construction in city parks; inspects and reviews effectiveness of programs; evaluates the performance of subordinates; helps prepare annual budget requests; makes reports.

Parks superintendent: Under the general direction of the director of parks and recreation, performs administrative duties to direct the planning, maintenance, and operation of all parks and recreational areas, facilities, buildings, and other public grounds. The parks superintendent reports to the director, who in turn reports to the city manager.

Several points can be made about these positions. First, the two lowest positions, gardeners and maintenance men, are those most directly involved in carrying out the stated purpose of the division. Second, those positions at higher levels and salaries tend to be described as under general supervision, and those at lower levels as under direct supervision. Reading "up" the hierarchy of job descriptions, few new specific tasks are added. (The exceptions in this example are that the foreman's job description adds the activities of installing a sprinkler system and requesting materials, and the parks maintenance supervisor helps prepare budget requests and makes reports.) Most of the new words attempt to convey status and responsibility for getting the work done *through* others; they are largely verbs such as supervising, evaluating, planning, and coordinating.

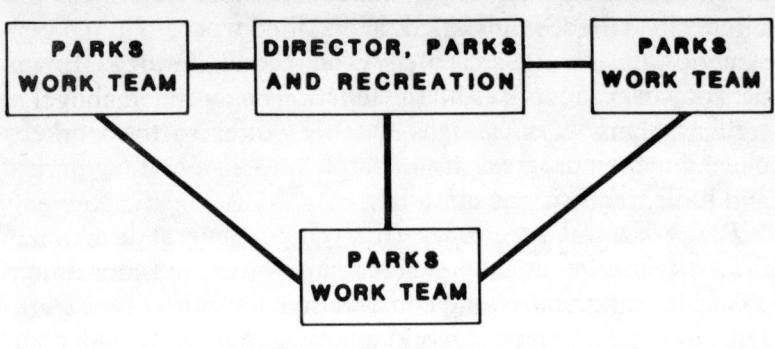

Figure 11.2 Proposed Modification of a Parks Division

THE REORGANIZATION

The job descriptions perpetuate and justify the hierarchy. Why, it may be asked, does the meaningful work of this division (the actual activities that meet the objectives described) require so much supervision? The answer proposed is that it does not. Under the proposed changes, the existing arrangement by which the city is divided into three geographical areas and a section or work group assigned to each area would be continued. These groups would be responsible for the maintenance and beautification of all the parks and city grounds in their area. The overall purpose of the division would remain the same. There would be no separate building repair section; these functions would be incorporated within the three groups organized geographically. A chart of the changed character of the Parks Division might look something like that shown in Figure 11.2.

Primary activities such as planting, trimming, cleaning, and building maintenance and repair would be divided among the members of each work team, in a manner they themselves choose, possibly based on interests, skills, and experience. They would probably elect to rotate functions to alleviate boredom or distaste with certain jobs. Primary attention of the groups would be on getting the work done in accordance with their agreed-on objectives. There would be no hierarchy of positions within the work groups.

Three liaison positions would be established in each team, and these would, like the other functions, be rotated among the team members. Possible duties attached to the first liaison position would be to maintain two-way communication with other teams, with Recreation and with the Parks and Recreation Director on all matters required to maintain the work group within the framework of the larger organization. This might include communication about organizational and team goals, the budget, and workers' pay and benefits.

The incumbent of the second liaison position might study or attend courses in order to acquire current information relating to horticulture and landscaping or other technical aspects of the team's work; this individual would keep other team members informed on a regular basis. The third liaison person might establish two-way communication with the public in the particular geographic area to identify their needs and preferences and to enlist the interest and support of those who use the parks.

It is proposed that there would be one director, as there is now, who would carry out functions similar to the descriptions found in the literature of what ideal or successful managers should do. Some of the proposed functions are undoubtedly similar to those now being performed by the incumbent of the director's position. These include: (1) facilitation of the flow of communication and coordination among the teams; (2) initiation and maintenance of communication with the "outside" environment (such as other city departments and the public) in an effort to determine whether or not there is a continuing need for the services provided, and continued feasibility in light of other objectives that must be met by the department or by the city as a whole; and (3) if need and feasibility continue, "managing" the actors and organizations in the environment who have influence on the Parks and Recreation Department in such a way that the work groups get the resources they need and are protected from unnecessary threats and interruptions in carrying out their tasks. In this particular organization, the director would also perform similar functions for the Recreation Division.

The preceding is not intended as a prescription for this or any other parks decision; it is intended to stimulate thinking about various ways of reducing the numbers and levels of supervision and of creating a structure utilizing self-management in a more or less typical line operation in local government. In this particular example, three "levels" of supervision would be removed; presumably more individuals would be involved in "doing" and fewer in "telling others to do so." The outcomes that can be expected are reduced salary costs, and, with cooperation as the key energizer, a gradual improvement and expansion in park services. The increased opportunities for individuals in the teams to assume responsibility and to create work assignments that interest them could be expected to generate an enthusiasm that would raise the quantity and quality of the work performed.

Example 2: A Public Assistance Agency

An example selected from a different field, social services, suggests that similar savings and improvement might be expected by allowing supervisors of workers in a public assistance agency to participate directly in determining the eligibility of applicants and in providing needed services to the recipients of benefits. To illustrate this, an existing county district office was selected; like other offices scattered over the county, it is mainly concerned with the implementation of programs such as Aid to Families with Dependent Children, Refugees, Medi-Cal, General Relief, and Food Stamps. The roles and duties of some of the personnel in this agency will be described briefly.

The district office is headed by a director, one of 34 in the large county department of which the district office is a part. (There are three levels of hierarchy above the position of director.) In the office described, there are four deputy district directors under the district director, only three of whom will be considered since the fourth is a deputy district director for administration heading a special section without a supervisor. Reporting to the three deputies are a total of 23 supervisors, and reporting to the supervisors are approximately 114 eligibility workers. (It it interesting to note the disparity between budgeted positions based on the recommended span of control, and the actual span of control. In this example, the budgeted ratios of deputy district director to supervisor is 1:10, and the existing average is 1:7.7. The budgeted ratio of supervisors for workers is 1:6 for intake and 1:7 for approved caseloads, whereas the average ratio for all supervisors to workers in this office is approximately 1:5.)

An examination of the job descriptions (or class specifications) of just two position levels, supervisor and eligibility worker, provides some of the information needed to assess the feasibility of reducing the amount of supervision in this office. Excluded from consideration are the five levels above the position of supervisor, even though it can safely be assumed that the work they perform might also benefit from a search for unnecessary supervision.

Supervisor. An incumbent of the supervisor's position is expected to supervise others in determining eligibility and benefits, and to refer problems requiring "social services" to social service staff. The incumbent will provide technical and administrative supervision to a unit of eligibility workers, plan, assign, supervise, and evaluate the work of the unit, train and instruct employees, review case records, discuss problem cases with eligibility workers, conduct unit meetings, and prepare or supervise the preparation of reports. (Interestingly, the class specification for the deputy district director, the "boss" of the supervisor, indicates that this individual is expected to do much the same thing, that is, assign, direct, and evaluate the work performed by eligibility workers except that this is to be accomplished *through* subordinate supervisors.)

Eligibility workers. Reading the job description of the eligibility worker is convincing evidence (at least to the outsider) that the duties attached to this position are the essence of the purposeful work of the office. Incumbents are expected to make initial and continuing eligibility and grant determinations for an assigned number of public assistance applicants or recipients. This includes interviewing applicants, interpreting provisions and limitations of the various assistance programs, analyzing financial and other eligibility information, computing benefits, and analyzing a client's social situation and providing support or referral if needed.

THE REORGANIZATION

In this public assistance office there are 23 separate units headed by a supervisor. If the 23 supervisors joined with the 114 workers in carrying out these essential functions, caseloads per worker would decrease, thus allowing (though not in itself ensuring) more time with clients and higher quality of service. This, of course, would require that the essential functions performed by the former supervisor be absorbed into the work of the units. The newly constituted cooperative teams could be expected to plan their own work, define tasks, assign and schedule duties, arrange flexible working hours, make reports as needed, discuss cases with special problems and decide if a referral is needed, establish special rotating liaison positions to ensure coordination with other teams and with the director, design quality control measures, adopt discipline procedures (whatever are available for discretionary action after formal policy is adhered to), and generally manage their own work in such a way that the maximum degree of individual choice and freedom is preserved.

This brief review of a public assistance office based on limited data obviously cannot suffice as a plan of action for this or any other organizational unit; as in the preceding example, it is intended to stimulate analyses of the particular variables involved in each unique situation, including the needs, preferences, and maturity of particular workers, and to raise questions about the necessity of existing levels of supervision. The work of this office differs in many ways from that performed in the parks example. Although they are no longer called social workers ("problem cases" are referred to the social service staff), the eligibility workers encounter individual and family crises and provide some counseling. In that sense, more discretion is built into their jobs, their work is less routine than that of some of the parks workers, and they work more with people, words, and paper than with tools. However, after allowing for these and other important differences between parks employees and public assistance workers, nothing in the nature of their respective activities as described appears to rule out the possibility of forming self-supervising teams or of simply eliminating some existing supervisorial positions.

Other Possible Applications of the Approach

Other governmental functions that might realize improvements based on this approach are trash collection, and the maintenance of streets, highways, automobiles, trucks, equipment, and buildings. Field offices of organizations such as the Department of Motor Vehicles, Social Security Administration, and the Internal Revenue Service might also benefit. In fact, candidates for experimenting with the approach described can be found in all those relatively large enclaves within government where often unglamorous but important work is performed under supervision. These are governmental units that typically have a hierarchy of positions, perform routine or repetitive tasks, and have large budgets.

The approach might also be applicable to functions such as law enforcement, probation, fire protection and control, education, and health care, as long as conditions unique to each are considered in modifying the approach. For example, in police, fire, and some health care facilities, work arrangements and role relationships need to accommodate the 24-hour nature of the service and to support an organizational structure that facilitates a quick response to crises. Cooperation and competency are always needed, but a strict and effective chain of command can save time and lives in an emergency.

In the case of probation, education, and health care (as well as in social welfare), the preponderance of personnel who are professionals, and the sentistive nonroutine nature of portions of their work (such as counseling or treating children, patients, and troubled adults), all require special attention when considering various forms of self-management. Sometimes, these professionals inside large bureaucracies are already quite autonomous in carrying out their duties, and the formation of work teams would not be a feasible alternative. The difficulty is that individuals who behave autonomously and perform satisfactorily may be encumbered by a supervisor in name only who makes little or no contribution to the quality of the work, but who absorbs a large salary and perpetuates the hierarchy. A general recommendation is that the identification of special considerations should not prevent the initiation of improvements in the top-heavy administrative systems and the unnecessary supervision often found in police, fire, and probation departments and in hospitals and school systems, to name just a few.

Problems of Implementation

These examples are not intended to convey a belief that the approach, even though modified to suit particular situations, will be easily accepted and implemented. Neither should it be assumed that following acceptance (should that occur), and with thoughtful planning and intelligent implementation, goal-directed work teams will emerge immediately as smoothly functioning, democratic bodies in which everyone is happy or even satisfied. New habit patterns will form slowly and probably painfully. What can be said at this stage is that the potential rewards appear to be greater than any that have emerged from the present proliferation of supervisorial layers.

Assuming for the moment that an organization thinks the approach has merit and wants to try it, the ideal situation would be one in which the approach would be part of a larger package that might include such improvements as a reduction in the adversary relationship between unions and management, improved relationships between government agencies and the legislative bodies that ostensibly provide policy guidelines and standards for them, more discretion for smaller units of government, and a host of other reforms that would bode well for the success of programs in which increased responsibility and autonomy are given to workers.

To wait for such a suitable environment to emerge is one strategy. Another is to move in the direction of reducing supervision whenever and however it is feasible, and simultaneously to work on other improvement goals. Because of the many pressures to reduce costs and streamline government, and because the presence of self-managing work groups may stimulate other kinds of needed changes, the recommendation here is to experiment with variations of the second strategy.

The Need for Managers

If one accepts the concept of self-management, the question arises as to whether managers or supervisors are necessary at all. It should be clear from the preceding examples that the answer proposed is a cautious yes, although in significantly fewer numbers than now exist. What is traditionally considered top management emerges as a still vital ingredient in organizational life, and to the extent that there is a trend toward viewing management as a process, with more emphasis on the functions and less on the prerogatives of individual managers, the climate for acceptance of the changes proposed in the study improves somewhat. For example, Mintzberg (1979) discusses the "strategic apex" of organizations, which he describes as having three major sets of duties: direct supervision, the management of the organization's boundary conditions, and the development of the organization's strategy. "In general, the strategic apex takes the widest, and as a result the most abstract, perspective of the organization. Work at this level is generally characterized by a minimum of repetition and standardization, considerable discretion, and relatively long decision-making cycles" (p. 26).

With the exception of direct supervision, the description given by Mintzberg tends to complement the recommendations presented earlier in this study with regard to what people at the top should do, and they bear restating here. In a system of self-managing work teams, examples of important functions that can probably best be performed by an intelligent, creative individual (or group of individuals) with a broad perspective and appreciation of the organization's mission are: (1) facilitating coordination among teams of workers; (2) creating a climate and means for reconciling emergent incompatibility of objectives of the various teams; (3) "minding" the external environment by evaluating the quality and quantity of the services produced by the organization, and by finding out whether the services continue to be valued by the recipients; and (4) dealing with actors and organizations in the environment in such a way that the work of the organization can proceed.

The excellent top executives or managers one can point to should be praised and encouraged to continue, but their presence should not hide nor excuse the fact that for every such executive in a large organization, there may be hundreds of persons labeled and paid as managers who not only perform largely unneeded functions, but who also interfere with the effective performance of others.

Public versus Private Sector Considerations

Although programs involving participative management and flexible work schedules have been cited in the public sector, the reported successes of self-management have occurred primarily in the private sector. While the phenomenon of the growing convergence of the two fields has been touched on in a previous chapter, skepticism about the applicability of various forms of self-management to the public sector is warranted on the basis that the profit-sharing motive introduced into many self-managing experiments in industry cannot be replicated in public organizations. However, a case can be made that some lower-level employees may "profit" if the work teams are non-hierarchical, and if the uniform salaries are based on savings resulting from the reduction in the numbers of managers. (This will be demonstrated shortly.)

Also, regardless of financial considerations, the general increase in worker satisfaction demonstrated in the private sector should be replicable; the giving up of such a well-learned habit as dependence on a boss can be expected to be traumatic, but the opportunity to determine work processes and to escape from unnecessary supervision may, after the initial shock, more than make up for the loss.

As for the external constraints, probably the greatest difference between public and private organizations in this regard is that the public agency faces more formidable obstacles than the private organization in the form of a complex network of laws, tradition, and intergovernmental relations. It is very likely that General Electric has more discretion to select a plant in which to reorganize dramatically the work and alter the superordinate/subordinate relationship than does, for example, the State of Massachusetts in a similar endeavor involving one of its agencies.

Factors Blocking and Facilitating the Approach

Although it is not feasible here to list all of the obstacles that come to mind when contemplating the reduction in the numbers and levels of managers and supervisors and the introduction of self-managing work teams, some of the more obvious are the unions, salary structuring, and other personnel policies, laws, administrative decrees, and traditions. Opposition to such changes can be expected from those who have a stake in the myth of management such as many managers, nonmanagers, consultants, and academicians in schools of management.

On the other hand, support for experimentation with a reduction in supervision can be discerned in the trend toward reducing the size of government, a workforce with increasing numbers of individuals who have new expectations concerning the quality of their working life, the negative public sentiment toward existing bureaucracies, a new philosophy of government being promulgated at the federal level, and most powerful of all (partly a consequence of the new philosophy under which priorities are being changed), a serious lack of resources with which to support government as we have known it.

Salaries

One of the obstacles mentioned earlier is that of existing salary structures. Nowhere is stratification in a given organization more visible than on wage and salary charts or tables. A discussion of a salary policy to match the objectives of the approach under consideration is likely to raise more antagonism than any other single issue, and it is tempting to avoid it altogether. By way of a compromise between a thorough analysis and complete avoidance, some very tentative ideas will be presented.

Perhaps a totally logical expression of the belief in the importance of doing over managing would be to reverse the traditional many-layered salary structure: those positions of doing (usually close to the bottom of the hierarchy) would receive the highest salary, thus introducing a new kind of incentive system in the interests of a more productive organization. However, it is unlikely that wide pay differentials for any purpose are conducive to the kind of cooperative labor imagined in this approach. Furthermore, the functions as described of the few remaining managers are sufficiently important, and require sufficiently more experience, wisdom, and perspective, to justify the highest salary. This concession would also serve to preserve a familiar vestige of the career ladder (or jump in this case), thereby reducing some of the resistance to experimenting with a self-managing approach.

However, to preserve the savings as well as the spirit of enlightened self-management, the differential would be very slight compared to current standards. It would seem reasonable, for example, to set the manager's salary (which would be the parks and recreation director in the first example) at a level 25 percent to 50 percent above that of the workers in the teams, all of whom would, in this example, be paid the same amount. Although groups with maximum feasible autonomy do not *require* uniform pay, it is congruent with the rotation of tasks and with the belief that each contribution will be as necessary as another in preparing the final product or service for which the group is responsible. This single salary should be set at as high a level as the organization can afford from the savings brought about by the reduced numbers of managers and supervisors and from the reduced salary disparity between the manager and the workers. One possible decision would be to pass along a share (perhaps 40 percent to 60 percent) of the savings as tax relief, while the remaining savings could be redistributed among the employees remaining.

In organizations with enormous budgets, the savings from one self-managing unit might seem small, particularly if the former supervisors joined the ranks of the worker rather than leaving the organization. However, the aggregated savings with a single large organization in which unnecessary supervision was eliminated from all its units would be substantial.

The redistribution of salaries is bound to cause problems of various kinds, one of which would result from the inevitable comparisons of what would be losses for some and gains for others. A gradual approach might ease some of the hardship; eventually, with some of the nonmonetary benefits becoming visible to the workers, and with growing reliance on cooperations, the distress over salary redistribution might subside. (In the parks example, assuming that 40 percent of the savings was considered as tax relief, that the manager receives 50 percent more than the uniform salary of the workers, and that the positions of superintendent, supervisor, and foreman were eliminated but the three individuals remained as workers, the salaries of those in the gardener 1 position and below would probably increase, while the others would decrease.)

Lest this discussion sound too far fetched, it should be pointed out that in one of the large departments in a county in California, many individuals have been demoted, with a loss of $500 or more per month. In spite of the painful individual adjustments, they (for the most part) continue to work, the hierarchy they criticize is preserved, and there are no recognizable benefits to other workers. By contrast, the decline in salary in accordance with a formula similar to the one suggested here would occur in a changed work environment. The rationale for the redistribution would be known by those taking a salary cut, and the pay loss for some and the gain for others could be judged within the context of the individual's experience with a radically new approach to work.

The prospect of actual experimentation with a self-managing approach brightens if it can be accomplished in organizations in which existing salary systems remain intact, and only functions are changed. Such experimentation might be feasible if the new work arrangements and role relationships were introduced on an interim basis for the purpose of making an initial assessment of the feasibility of self-management in carrying out the work of the organizational unit. However, in order to meet the objective of reducing cost, and in order to assess the influence of salary differential on performance, this demonstration period would necessarily be followed by some method of either gradually eliminating some management or supervisorial classifications, but keeping the same number of employees and easing out pay differentials among them, or by deleting the positions and laying off their incumbents. In some cases, those facing reduced status or salary will voluntarily seek work elsewhere.

Summary

Two examples have been given of organizational subunits and of what might be accomplished through work redesign that would establish self-managing work groups in lieu of some of the existing supervision. It is assumed that the implementation of the approach described would not necessarily require layoffs but would involve multiple reassignment of the existing workforce, primarily in the direction of more doing kinds of activities. As stated earlier, the examples, along with the discussion of drastic changes in salary structures, should not deter those who are critical of both excessive supervision and of self-managing models (particularly if they involve uniform pay) from eliminating unneeded supervisorial and management positions. However, judging by the many positive experiences with work redesign programs in which semi-autonomous work groups are formed, there is reason to believe that programs that foster greater autonomy for workers can create an improved quality of working life and promote greater organizational effectiveness. The approach described in this chapter attempts to combine cost saving with quality of life benefits.

Whether reforms of this nature are mild or radical, it seems likely that there will be an initial departure of some of the former managers and supervisors unwilling to give up their status and salaries, or unwilling to wait for the projected layoffs. Some bright, young, ambitious people might also leave due to the reduced possibilities of advancement; if the changes involved more than just depletion of supervisorial positions, the few remaining managers would face the difficult task of reeducating the workforce to a different philosophy of work and of training some in the specific skills needed by work teams.

Eventually, it might be expected that different incentives, such as self-goverance, opportunities for innovation, greater flexibility of working hours, and more interesting jobs might replace the old ones of promotion and salary increments, and that some bright young people (part of the new breed) whose chief goals are neither large salaries nor advancement might be attracted to the organization. Since much of the effort in adjusting would involve overcoming former attitudes and habits and vested interests, introducing this or a similar approach to a newly formed organization would be somewhat easier than changing an existing, well-entrenched one. In either case, however, it would not be easy.

The approach outlined in this chapter is general in nature and cannot be prescriptive for any particular organization. It is intended primarily to stimulate interest on the part of those who agree philosophically with the underlying premises, and who know a particular organization well enough to find specific ways to reduce unnecessary management and supervision. There are enormous varieties of public organizations, each of whose existing structure, mandate, degree of discretion, tasks, technology, and major purposes would inevitably dictate the extent to which it could experiment with any kind of work redesign.

CONCLUSION

While some writers predict the demise or withering away of large bureaucracies, the prevailing view seems to be that they are here to stay, possibly with increased abilities to respond to the ubiquitous "complex environment." Some believe they will grow larger, but worry about the limits to complexity and whether bureaucracies are becoming unmanageable (Elgin & Bushnell, 1977). Many argue that they will become more and more centralized. "For all the talk of flat organizations these days, we are witnessing even more strenuous efforts to peak authority. In part, this may be understood in terms of the growth in organizational size and complexity—which intensifies both the problem of uncertainty and the impulse toward control" (Landau & Stout, 1979, p. 151). A clear statement of what seems to be the prevailing view is that "bureaucracy is the inevitable handmaiden of large-scale technology, and it is unlikely that post-industrial society will do other than magnify the bureaucratic phenomenon" (Jaques, 1976, p. 376). As for the future role of managers in these inevitable bureaucracies, the prediction for the year 2001 that "future organizational growth will call for more managers" (Bass & Ryterband, 1973/1977, p. 401) seems to sum up the views of most writers.

Given the likely continuation of large-scale government organizations, what, on balance, are the probabilities that work redesign efforts will expand? Some optimists who favor self-management may look for a natural evolution from, for example, participative management toward an approach such as that described in this study. An important goal shared by both work redesign and participative management programs is to enhance effectiveness and to improve quality of working life through increased participation by subordinates in decision making.

However, those managers who adopt a participative style typically do so with the clear intention of retaining (although softening a bit), the hierarchical structure of the organization. They point with pride to the fact that they must always and inevitably assume authority and responsibility for final decisions, regardless of how much participation subordinates are allowed. By contrast, self-management in the approach proposed eliminates the need for many management and supervisorial positions and alters the basic hierarchical nature of authority.

There are signs of a revitalized interest in participative management that may in time create a climate in which there is greater acceptance of self-managing models. Quality circles, for example, are receiving a great deal of attention as a new idea, and have enjoyed success in both public and private organizations. (Not too long ago, a very similar activity was identified as participant action research, "in which the people who are to take action are involved in the entire research and action process from the beginning" [French & Bell, 1973, p. 94].) Much like the action research teams, quality circles are usually groups of from eight to ten people who meet regularly to identify and solve work-related problems. After this "research" stage, they submit their recommendations to management, and in some cases carry the recommendations, once approved, into action.

One of the advantages of quality circles is that their work is structured, and it is less likely that organizations can ignore their existence; some managers are prone to forgetfulness when there is merely a general commitment to participative management but no provision for any ongoing, systematic process. For many, another advantage is that QCs do not, in themselves, require any change in the formal structure of work or in formal role relationships. A tentative conclusion is that, to the extent that quality circles and other forms of participative management are successful in moving decisions about work down to the level of the natural work units where essential activities are carried out, and to the extent that these decision-making processes become an integral part of the organizations, they may become (for those interested in more basic reforms) a foot in the door for self-management.

This optimism is diminished somewhat by a number of personal experiences in public organizations. Many forms of participative management or worker participation utilize the talents and ingenuity of the workers on behalf of management, while at the same time carefully preserving the separation of roles, retaining the layers of supervision, and ensuring traditional management control over the work and over subordinates. There is a significant difference between, on the one hand, being invited by management to help make decisions or to serve as advisers by identifying problems and solutions for management, and on the other hand, working cooperatively with others in a self-managing group in which the primary purpose of communication with top management is not to suggest or to recommend, but to keep top management informed about decisions made by the group and to ensure coordination with the work going on in other self-managing groups.

It must be concluded that the most optimistic prediction about the proposition under consideration is that largely because of factors mentioned earlier—pressures to reduce spending, the "getting government off our backs" syndrome, a nongrowing public sector with reduced promotion possibilities, scarce resources, employees' ability to perform their work without supervision, and lack of managerial discretion to justify the higher management salaries—a few individuals, or groups, or even the taxpayers may begin to question the utility of managers and supervisors and to seek opportunities to change their functions or reduce their numbers. However, if they decide to reduce government only under pressure to reduce costs, they are likely to create smaller replicas of existing structures, which would be likely to perpetuate the unnecessary supervision, the low quality of working life, and the poor government services that some believe are the result of such structures. Workers will continue to suffer from oversupervision where little or none is needed, and the myth of the appropriate domination of manager over worker will continue.

If, on the other hand, these individuals or groups, still responding to public pressure, are willing to question the necessity of managers and supervisors on the grounds that it may be a fiction based more on traditional vested interests and convenience than on fact, and that it may unnecessarily suppress human creativity, a new foundation for experimentation will have been established. The hypothesis to be tested is that saving public money and improving the quality of working life are synergistic objectives that, when achieved, seem likely to result in improvements in public service. An optimistic prediction is that the results of such experiments, rather than the myth of management, will eventually help determine the form of future government organizations.

APPENDIX A
Survey of Public Managers
(background notes)

Development of the Questionnaire

A preliminary questionnaire was designed in October 1978, and pretests were initiated in November 1978, with managers and nonmanagers. Both the form and substance of the questionnaire underwent a series of pretests and revisions from January to March of 1979. Approximately 55 managers and nonmanagers completed questionnaires on a pretest basis. There were seven major revisions, resulting in a final format in April 1979. The general trends in the revisions were: (a) from including a mix of items requiring a written verbal response and items requiring numerical responses toward exclusive use of the latter; (b) from utilizing lists of fairly detailed activities toward a mix of specific kinds of activities and general broad categories of activities; and (c) from asking about changes in managers' activities over time to asking only about current (within the past year) activities. (The pretest responses to items estimating time spent on categories of activities in the past five years, at present, and five years in the future revealed virtually no variance.)

Questionnaire Distribution

A variety of agencies (federal, state, and municipal) were selected to participate in the survey. After an agency had agreed to participate, instructions for distributing and returning the questionnaires were given by telephone. This personal contact appeared to facilitate the successful completion of the survey and provided an opportunity to explain that it was important to obtain information about what managers do from managers themselves as well as from those who work with or for them. Since not all positions fall clearly within one or the other category, two general distinctions were offered to agency representatives in case there was a problem as to which form to give to whom. One method suggested was to distinguish between those who primarily give supervision to, or have responsibility for others (managers), and those who primarily receive supervision (nonmanagers). This instruction reduced but did not eliminate the ambiguity. (Many managers both give and receive supervision, and there are many nonsupervisory positions at high levels of the organization that are very much like management positions.) The other suggestion was that anyone generally considered "part of management" should complete the manager's questionnaire.

Unlike the convention in most organizations, and in most studies, first-line supervisors were asked to complete the manager's form. Positions commonly referred to as foreman or leadman were excluded from the management group in oral and written instructions to participating agencies. The rationale for this decision was that in many organizations, the foreman and leadman are working or doing supervisors, while the first-line supervisor increasingly is responsible for at least two levels below, i.e., foreman and laborers, thereby pushing him or her higher in the hierarchy. Also excluded from the management group were all secretarial and clerical positions, in spite of the fact that many individuals in those positions supervise others.

Although the reason for having two questionnaires originally grew out of the need to gain perceptual data about what managers do from more than one source, it became clear as the questionnaire was being designed and pretested that data from nonmanagers would be more useful in analyzing the particular function of supervision than in contrasting or corroborating the two perceptions of managers' functions in general.

More specific information about survey results can be found in Appendixes B, C, and D.

APPENDIX B
Summary of Managers' Responses to Survey Items by Type of Agency

The following is a summary of the characteristics of managers who participated in a survey in 1979, and their mean responses to all questionnaire items, by type of agency.

Characteristics of Managers

	Number of Persons
(1) Position Category	
(a) Top management	44
(b) Middle management	74
(c) First line supervisor	59
(d) Assistant or staff to a management position	5
(e) Other	3
Total managers participating	185

	Number of Managers
(2) Types of Organizations	
(a) Federal "mix." (This included a variety of agencies such as Labor, Defense, FAA, Commerce, Customs, and Transportation.)	11
(b) A single office of a large federal agency	8
(c) Several offices of a single state agency (California)	95
(d) Ten California cities	71
	185

(continued)

	Mean			
	All Managers	Cities	State	Federal
(3) Years in the Position	4	5	4	4
(4) Years in the Organization	12	9	15	12
(5) Number of persons Employed in the Manager's Unit	65	115	35	31

	Mean Response			
	All Managers	Cities	State	Federal*
(1) Percentage of total work time spent in meetings in the past year	20	25	14	23
(2) Overall effectiveness or productiveness of meetings (1 = low; 9 = high)	6.4	6.8	6.3	6.0

	(F)	(I)	(F)	(I)	(F)	(I)	(F)	(I)
(3) Frequency (F) and Importance (I) of activities. (1 = not at all frequent or important; 9 = very frequent or important.)								
(a) Supervision	6.7	7.7	6.0	7.3	7.0	7.9	6.7	7.6
(b) Budget	3.8	6.3	5.5	7.7	2.6	5.4	3.0	4.9
(c) Employee relations	5.7	7.6	5.9	7.7	5.6	7.6	5.3	7.0
(d) Conflict resolution	4.2	7.6	4.4	7.3	3.8	7.7	5.3	7.4
(e) Policy development	4.5	7.2	5.5	7.9	3.7	6.7	4.5	6.8

Mean Response

	All Managers		Cities		State		Federal*	
(f) Policy implementation or coordination	6.1	7.6	6.1	7.8	5.9	7.4	6.6	7.5
(g) Self-development (training or education)	4.2	6.9	4.4	7.4	4.3	6.8	3.3	5.7
(h) Routine paperwork	6.2	4.9	6.2	4.9	6.4	5.1	5.6	4.3
(i) Contacts with secretary	5.3	5.9	6.4	6.8	4.3	5.3	5.5	6.0
(j) Contacts with subordinates	7.5	7.9	7.0	7.6	7.9	8.2	7.6	8.1
(k) Contacts with boss	5.9	7.6	5.6	7.8	6.3	7.6	5.6	7.0
(l) Contacts with unions	1.9	3.1	2.6	4.0	1.3	8.2	2.8	4.0
(m) Contacts with other governmental agencies	3.8	5.4	4.6	6.4	3.0	7.6	4.2	6.2
(n) Contacts with the business community	3.6	5.2	4.1	5.8	3.4	2.2	2.3	3.7
(o) Contacts with the public	5.4	7.0	5.8	7.4	5.4	4.6	3.5	5.5
(p) Contacts with policy, legislative, advisory, or regulatory bodies	3.1	5.4	4.3	6.4	2.1	4.9	2.9	4.5
(q) Contacts with the press or other media	2.4	4.5	3.2	5.6	1.8	7.1	2.2	2.8
(r) Contacts with other managers	5.3	6.7	5.5	6.9	5.2	6.7	5.0	6.8

(continued)

MANAGING WITHOUT MANAGERS

	Mean Response			
	All Managers	Cities	State	Federal*
(4) Percentage of total work time spent in the past on major categories of activities				
(a) Planning	30	31	29	34
(b) Organizing	28	29	27	27
(c) Controlling	41	39	43	39
(d) Maintenance	63	59	67	56
(e) Development	37	41	32	43
(f) Internal	67	57	74	57
(g) Enlarged	19	16	19	27
(h) External	13	27	06	16

	Mean Response			
	All Managers	Cities	State	Federal
(5) Organizational characteristics (1 = none at all; 9 = a great deal)				
(a) Extent to which work in the organization is routine	6.1	5.6	6.5	5.9
(b) Extent to which work depends on technical skill	6.4	6.5	6.4	5.8
(c) Extent to which the organization is autonomous or independent	3.4	3.9	2.9	3.3

	Mean Response			
	All Managers	Cities	State	Federal*
(6) Amount of discretion of the individual manager in the following activities (1 = none at all; 9 = a great deal)				
(a) Hiring	5.5	6.3	5.0	5.0
(b) Promoting	4.8	6.1	3.6	5.4
(c) Firing	4.4	5.7	3.5	3.6
(d) Improving efficiency	6.6	7.5	6.1	6.0
(e) Improving effectiveness	6.8	7.5	6.3	6.5
(f) Formulating purposes, objectives, goals	4.7	6.8	3.3	3.6
(7) Supervision (1 = none at all; 9 = a great deal)				
(a) Extent of influence on the performance of subordinates	7.1	7.3	7.1	6.4
(b) Extent of improvement if subordinates received:				
More supervision	4.0	4.4	3.8	3.5
Less supervision	2.5	2.6	2.4	2.6
Different kind of supervision	3.9	4.2	2.4	2.4
No supervision	1.9	1.8	1.9	2.1
One or more additional supervisors	3.0	3.3	2.5	2.9

(continued)

	Mean Response			
	All Managers	*Cities*	*State*	*Federal**
(8) Probability of various consequences occurring if the manager's position was unfilled for one year (1 = very low probability; (9 = very high probability)				
(a) Manager's functions would be reduced in number and dispersed throughout the organization	4.0	4.1	3.9	3.7
(b) Functions shifted to others higher in the organization	3.7	4.1	3.5	3.6
(c) Functions shifted to others lower in the organization	5.3	5.7	5.4	3.5
(d) Functions given to another manager at the same level	4.9	3.8	5.2	6.1
(e) Functions would not be performed	1.9	2.7	1.5	2.1
(f) Secretary would continue correspondence, take care of minor but urgent matters, and hold other work until return	1.7	2.5	1.2	2.6

* In computing this mean response, the federal "mix" and the single office of a large federal agency were combined.

APPENDIX C
Summary of Nonmanagers' Responses to Survey Items by Type of Agency

	Mean Percentage of Time							
	All Non-Managers		Cities		State		Federal	
	(A)	(S)	(A)	(S)	(A)	(S)	(A)	(S)
(1) Actual (A) time spent by supervisors on major categories of activities vs. time they should (S) spend								
(a) Planning	31	33	30	33	33	32	24	36
(b) Organizing	29	30	32	31	26	29	30	32
(c) Controlling	39	36	37	35	40	39	45	31

	Mean Response			
	All Non-Managers	Cities	State	Federal
(2) Unit characteristics (1 = none at all; 9 = a great deal)				
(a) Extent to which work in the unit is routine	5.9	5.7	6.4	4.4
(b) Extent to which work depends on technical skills	4.9	5.2	4.8	5.5

(continued)

	Mean Response			
	All Non-Managers	Cities	State	Federal
(c) Extent to which unit is autonomous or independent	4.0	4.5	3.6	4.1
(3) Amount of discretion of the supervisor in the following activities (1 = none at all; 9 = a great deal)				
(a) Formulating purpose, objectives, and goals of the unit	5.9	6.4	5.5	6.5
(b) Hiring	6.1	6.4	6.0	5.1
(c) Promoting	5.1	5.6	4.7	5.8
(d) Firing	5.2	6.0	4.6	5.3
(4) Supervision (1 = none; 9 = a great deal)				
(a) Extent to which the supervisor influences the performance of the nonmanager	5.7	5.8	5.6	5.8
(b) Amount of present work assignment that could be completed without supervision	7.7	7.7	7.8	7.7
(c) Effect of various changes in supervision on the effectiveness of the unit, the individual nonmanager's satisfaction, and others' satisfaction (0 = no effect; − 9 = great decrease in effectiveness or satisfaction; + 9 = great increase in effectiveness or satisfaction)				

Appendix C

	Unit effectiveness (Mean)			
	All Non-Managers	Cities	State	Federal
More supervision	+1.0	+1.4	+1.1	−1.3
No supervision	−3.2	−3.5	−3.3	−0.1
No supervisor	−4.4	−4.5	−4.6	−2.4
Less supervision	−1.5	−2.0	−1.5	+1.5
Additional supervisors	−2.8	−2.7	−2.6	−5.4
A different supervisor	−0.8	−1.5	−0.1	−1.1

	Individual Nonmanagers Satisfaction (Mean)			
	All Non-Managers	Cities	State	Federal
More supervision	+0.05	+0.43	+0.15	−2.4
No supervision	−1.9	−2.5	−1.9	+0.75
No supervisor	−2.7	−2.8	−2.8	−0.75
Less supervision	−0.15	−0.69	−0.14	+2.7
Additional supervisors	−3.5	−3.5	−3.1	−6.0
A different supervisor	−1.1	−1.9	−0.43	−0.85

	Others' Satisfaction (Mean)			
	All Non-Managers	Cities	State	Federal
More supervision	+0.59	+4.4	+0.82	−2.0
No supervision	−2.3	−5.8	−2.5	+0.72
No supervisor	−3.4	−6.6	−3.5	−1.2
Less supervision	−1.1	−5.8	−1.6	+1.3
Additional supervisors	−3.2	−4.8	−2.9	−5.7
A different supervisor	−0.63	+2.2	−0.12	−0.20

(continued)

	Mean Response			
	All Non-Managers	*Cities*	*State*	*Federal*

(5) Consequences of various alternatives in the event that the supervisor's position remains unfilled for one year (1 = very unfavorable consequences; 9 = very favorable consequences)

(a) Functions of the supervisor would be reduced in number and dispersed throughout the organization	3.7	3.8	3.6	3.9
(b) Functions shifted higher in the organization	3.6	3.1	3.9	3.5
(c) Functions shifted lower in the organization	4.4	4.9	4.1	3.4
(d) Functions given to another manager at the same level	4.9	4.5	5.5	4.7
(e) Functions would not be performed	1.7	1.7	1.9	1.3
(f) Secretary would continue correspondence, take care of minor but urgent matters, and hold other work until supervisor returns	2.8	2.8	3.1	1.6

APPENDIX D
Effects of Changes in Supervision as Rated by Nonmanagers

	Unit Effectiveness (Mean)	Nonmgrs' Satisfaction (Mean)	Others' Satisfaction (Mean)
More supervision from your supervisor	−1.0 (151)	+0.1 (150)	+0.6 (149)
No supervision from your supervisor	−3.2 (152)	−1.9 (150)	−2.3 (149)
No supervisor	−4.4 (152)	−2.7 (150)	−3.4 (149)
Less supervision from your supervisor	−1.5 (152)	−0.1 (150)	−1.1 (149)
Additional supervisors	−2.8 (152)	−3.5 (149)	−3.2 (148)
A different supervisor	−0.7 (148)	−1.1 (148)	−0.6 (145)

NOTE: In parentheses are the numbers of nonmanagers responding. The scale used by respondents was −9 = great decrease (in effectiveness or satisfaction); 0 = no change; +9 = great increase (in effectiveness or satisfaction).

REFERENCES

ACIR identifies public sector slowdown. *Public Administration Times,* January 15, 1982, p. 5.

Alber, A. F. Job enrichment programs seen improving employee performance, but benefits not without cost. *World of Work Report,* January 1978, pp. 8-11.

Argyris, C. Some characteristics of successful executives. *The Personnel Journal,* 1953, *32*(1), 50-55.

Barnard, C. I. *The functions of the executive.* Cambridge, MA: Harvard University Press, 1954. (Originally published, 1938.)

Bass, B. M., & Ryterband, E. C. Work and organizational life in 2001. In J. M. Ivancevich, A. D. Szilagyi, Jr., & M. J. Wallace, Jr. (Eds.), *Readings in organizational behavior and performance.* Santa Monica, CA: Goodyear, 1977. (Originally published, 1973.)

Benveniste, G. *Bureaucracy.* San Francisco: Boyd & Fraser, 1977.

Bowman, J. S. Managerial Theory and Practice: The Transfer of Knowledge in Public Administration. *Public Administration Review,* 1978, *38,* 563-570.

Braverman, H. *Labor and monopoly capital* New York: Monthly Review Press, 1974.

Bucklow, M. A new role for the work group. In J. M. Ivancevich, A. D. Szilagyi, Jr., & M. J. Wallace, Jr. (Eds.), *Readings in organizational behavior and performance.* Santa Monica, CA: Goodyear, 1977. (Originally published, 1966).

Burnham, J. *The managerial revolution.* Bloomington: Indiana University Press, 1960. (Originally published, 1941.)

Buying jobs. *Time,* December 24, 1979, p. 39.

Candid reflections of a business man in Washington. *Fortune,* January 29, 1979, pp. 36-49.

Caplow, T. *How to run any organization.* New York: Holt, Rinehart & Winston, 1976.

Carlson, S. *Executive behaviour: A study of the work load and the working methods of managing directors.* Stockholm: Strombergs, 1951.

Casner-Lotto, J. Participation teams "work" at a Jones and Laughlin plant. *World of Work Report,* February 1982, pp. 9; 10-11. (a)

Casner-Lotto, J. Labor-management teamwork boosts morale and "profits." *World of Work Report,* August 1982, pp. 57; 61-62. (b)

Casner-Lotto, J. Labor-management groups spawn new QWL programs. *World of Work Report,* September 1982, pp. 65-67. (c)

References

Clark, T. D., Jr., & Shrode, W. A. Public sector decision structures: An empirically-based description. *Public Administration Review,* 1979, *39,* 343-354.

Cooper, M. R., Morgan, B. S., Foley, P. M., & Kaplan, L. B. Changing employee values: Deepening discontent? *Harvard Business Review,* January-February 1979, pp. 117-125.

Cummings, T. G., Molloy, E. S. *Improving productivity and the quality of work life.* New York: Praeger, 1977.

Crozier, M. *The bureaucratic phenomenon.* Chicago: University of Chicago Press, 1964.

Drucker, P. *The practice of management.* New York: Harper & Row, 1954.

Drucker, P. *Management: Tasks, responsibilities, practices.* New York: Harper & Row, 1974.

Edwards, R. *Contested terrain.* New York: Basic Books, 1979.

Elgin, D. S., & Bushnell, R. A. The limits to complexity: Are bureaucracies becoming unmanageable? *The Futurist,* December 1977, pp. 337-348.

Encouraging employee ownership: A new role for the states. *World of Work Report,* January 1982, pp. 6-7.

Endicott, W. Tax hikes are expected, hope is for budget cuts. *Los Angeles Times,* November 10, 1981, pp. 1; 21.

Fayol, H. *Administration industrielle et genèrale.* Paris: Dunod, 1950. (Originally published, 1916.)

Follett, M. P. *Dynamic Administration* (H. C. Metcalf & L. Urwick, Eds.). New York: Harper & Brothers, 1940.

Freeman, R. B. The work force of the future: An overview. In C. Kerr & J. Rosow (Eds.), *Work in America: The decade ahead.* New York: Van Nostrand Reinhold, 1979.

French, W. L., & Bell, C. H., Jr. *Organization development.* Englewood Cliffs, NJ: Prentice-Hall, 1973.

General Accounting Office of the United States. Report to the Congress. *The alternative work schedules experiment: Congressional oversight needed to avoid likely failure* (November 14, 1980, B-200409). Washington, DC: GAO.

General Accounting Office of the United States. Report to the Congress. *Employment trends and grade controls in the DOD general schedule workforce* (July 28, 1981, B-203027). Washington, DC: GAO.

Gulick, L. H. Notes on the theory of organization. In L. H. Gulick & L. F. Urwick (Eds.), *Papers on the science of administration.* New York: Columbia University Press, 1937.

Hackman, J. R. Work redesign. In J. R. Hackman & J. L. Suttle (Eds.), *Improving life at work.* Santa Monica, CA: Goodyear, 1977. (Portions originally published, 1975.)

Hersey, P. & Blanchard, K. H. *Management of organizational behavior: Utilizing human resources.* Englewood Cliffs, NJ: Prentice-Hall, 1977.

Ivancevich, J. M., Szilagyi, A. D., Jr., & Wallace, M. J., Jr. *Organizational behavior and performance.* Santa Monica, CA: Goodyear, 1977.

Jaques, E. *A general theory of bureaucracy.* New York: Halstead, 1976.

Johnston, D. Council votes to phase out 18 top police department jobs. *Los Angeles Times,* January 27, 1982, pp. 1; 3.

Katz, D., & Kahn, R. L. *The social psychology of organizations.* New York: John Wiley, 1966.

Katz, R. L. Skills of an effective administrator. *Harvard Business Review,* September-October 1974, pp. 90-102. (Originally published, 1955.)

Katzell, R. A. Changing attitudes toward work. In C. Kerr & J. M. Rosow (Eds.), *Work in America: The decade ahead.* New York: Van Nostrand Reinhold, 1979.

Katzell, R. A., Barrett, R. S., Vann, D. H., & Hogan, J. M. Organizational correlates of executive roles. *Journal of Applied Psychology,* 1968, *52,*(1), 22-28.

Kurke, L. B. & Aldrich, H. E. *Mintzberg was right!: A replication and extension of the nature of managerial work.* Paper presented at the 39th Annual Meeting of the Academy of Management, Atlanta, August 10, 1979.

Landau, M., & Stout, R., Jr. To manage is not to control: Or the folly of type II errors. *Public Administration Review,* 1979, *39,* 148-156.

Lau, A. W., Newman, A. R., & Broedling, L. A. The Nature of managerial work in the public sector. *Public Administration Review,* 1980, *40,* 513-520.

Law, J. M. Quality circles at a naval shipyard: Employee involvement ups productivity. *World of Work Report,* January 1981, pp. 3-4.

Lindblom, C. E. The science of muddling through. *Public Administration Review,* 1959, *19,* 79-88.

Lindblom, C. E. *The policy making process.* Englewood Cliffs, NJ: Prentice-Hall, 1968.

Los Angeles County Economy and Efficiency Commission. *Eliminating automatic step increases and controlling supervisory costs in Los Angeles County government.* Report by the Task Force on Management and Finances of the Los Angeles County Economy and Efficiency Commission, September 1976.

Mars, D. *What's ahead: A look at local government in the greater Los Angeles area, 1981-2001.* Working Paper, USC School of Public Administration. (Published in cooperation with the Public Policy Institute of the Center for Public Affairs, 1980-1981/48).

Martin, S. *Assessment of organizational and training needs.* Unpublished report, 1978. (a)

Martin, S. *In support of discrimination on behalf of employees of public organizations.* Unpublished report, 1978. (b)

Martin, S. *An assessment of attitudes, issues, and training needs.* Unpublished report, 1979.

Martin, S. *The functions of public managers.* Unpublished Doctoral Dissertation, University of Southern California, 1981.

McCurdy, H. E. Selecting and training public managers: Business skills versus public administration. *Public Administration Review,* 1978, *38,* 571-578.

McCurdy, H. E. RIFS fall unevenly in federal agencies. *Public Administration Times,* January 15, 1982, pp. 1; 10.

McGregor, D. *The human side of enterprise.* New York: McGraw-Hill, 1960.

McWhinney, W., & Krone, C. *Open systems planning.* Unpublished manuscript, 1972. (Available from Enthusion, Venice, California.)

Mintzberg, H. *The nature of managerial work.* New York: Harper & Row, 1973.
Mintzberg, H. The manager's job: Folklore and fact. *Harvard Business Review,* July-August 1975, pp. 49-61.
Mintzberg, H. *The structuring of organizations.* Englewood Cliffs, NJ: Prentice-Hall, 1979.
Olsen, D. A work improvement project enhances QWL in public sector. *World of Work Report,* April 1982, pp. 25-27.
Organizational, wage system changes boost productivity at Volkswagen's auto repair shops in Stockholm. *World of Work Report,* January 1978, pp. 4-5.
Parkinson, C. N. Parkinson's law or the rising pyramid. In J. M. Shafritz & A. C. Hyde (Eds.), *Classics of public administration.* Oak Park, IL: Moore Publishing, 1978. (Originally published 1957.)
Pascal, A. H., Menchik, M. D., Chaiken, J. M., Ellickson, P. L., Walker, W. E., De Tray, D. N., & Wise, A. E. *Fiscal containment of local and state government.* Santa Monica, CA: Rand Corporation, September 1979. (R-2494-FF/RC)
Perrow, C. *Complex organizations.* Glenview, IL: Scott, Foresman, 1972.
Plous, F. K., Jr. The quality circle concept: Growing by leaps and bounds. *World of Work Reports,* April 1981, pp. 25-27.
Quality circles boost productivity in North Carolina's state offices. *World of Work Report,* September 1981, pp. 65; 67-68.
Ramos, A. G. *The new science of organizations.* Toronto: University of Toronto Press, 1981.
Rosow, J. M. Quality-of-work-life issues for the 1980's. In C. Kerr & J. M. Rosow (Eds.), *Work in America: The decade ahead.* New York: Van Nostrand Reinhold, 1979.
Rosow, J. M. A new direction for labor: Quality of working life. *World of Work Report,* March 1982, pp. 17-19.
Rosow, J. M., & Zager, R. *New work schedules for a changing society.* A Work in America Institute Policy Study. New York: Work in America Institute, 1981.
Salzmann, R. R. *The world of change: Some added notes for management.* Conference address at the California Institute of Technology, 1969.
Sayles, L. R. *Managerial behavior: Administration in complex organizations.* New York: Robert E. Krieger, 1980. (Originally published, 1964.)
Self-managed teams at Butler plant cut costs, raise profitability. *World of Work Report,* November 1977, pp. 124-126.
Selznick, P. *Leadership in administration.* New York: Row, Peterson, 1957.
Shartle, C. L. *Executive performance and leadership.* Englewood Cliffs. NJ: Prentice-Hall, 1956.
Simon, H. A. *Administrative behavior.* New York: Free Press, 1976.
Soyka, D. Honeywell pioneers in quality circle movement. *World of Work Report,* September 1981, pp. 65-67.
Spanish industrial cooperatives achieve a remarkable success. *World of Work Report,* November 1977, pp. 129-131.
Statistical abstract of the United States. Washington, DC: Bureau of the Census, 1981.
Stryker, P. On the meaning of executive qualities. *Fortune,* June 1958, pp. 116-119; 186; 189.

Taylor, J. C. Job satisfaction and quality of working life: A reassessment. *Occupational Psychology,* 1977, *50,* 243-252.

Taylor, F. W. *The principles of scientific management.* New York: Harper & Brothers, 1934. (Originally published, 1911.)

Thompson, J. *Organizations in action.* New York: McGraw-Hill, 1967.

Treadwell, D. Public sector jobs drop for 1st time in 35 years. *Los Angeles Times,* December 31, 1981.

Trist, E. *A socio-technical critique of scientific management.* Paper presented at the Edinburgh Conference on the Impact of Science and Technology, May 1970.

U.S. Office of Personnel Management, Office of Productivity Policy Analysis. *A statistical profile of the federal civilian workforce, 1968-1979.* June 1980. Washington, DC: OPM.

Wallace, A. M. Labor-management QWL program "works" at a Shell chemical plant. *World of Work Report,* February 1981, pp. 11-12.

Walton, R. E. Improving the quality of work life. *Harvard Business Review,* May-June 1974, pp. 12; 16; 155.

Webber, R. A. *Management: Basic elements of managing organizations.* Homewood, IL: Richard D. Irwin, 1979.

Work in America. Report by a special task force to the Secretary of Health, Education and Welfare. Cambridge: MIT Press, 1973.

Wrapp, H. E. Good managers don't make policy decisions. *Harvard Business Review,* September-October 1967, pp. 91-99.

Yankelovich, D. Work, values, and the new breed. In C. Kerr & J. M. Rosow (Eds.), *Work in America: The decade ahead.* New York: Van Nostrand Reinhold, 1979.

Zaleznik, A. Power and politics in organizational life. In D. R. Hampton, C. E. Summer, & R. A. Webber (Eds.), *Organizational behavior and the practice of management.* Glenview, IL: Scott, Foresman, 1973. (Originally published, 1970.)

NAME INDEX

Alber, A. F., 112
Aldrich, H. E., 24, 63
Argyris, C., 25
Barnard, C. I., 39, 71-75, 79
Barrett, R. S., 23
Bass, B. M., 145-146, 173
Bell, C. H., 174
Benveniste, G., 138
Blanchard, K. H., 27, 144, 145
Bowman, J. S., 39
Braverman, H., 44, 45, 46, 47, 77, 98-99, 102, 137, 146
Broedling, L. A., 24, 37, 144
Bucklow, M., 105-106
Burham, J., 43
Bushnell, R. A., 88, 90, 144, 173
Caplow, T., 149
Carlson, S., 22
Casner-Lotto, J., 113, 120, 121
Chaiken, J. M., 53-54
Clark, T. D., Jr., 92-93, 144
Cooper, M. R., 102
Cummings, T. G., 103, 105
Crozier, M., 111
Drucker, P., 19, 21, 26, 39, 46
Edwards, R., 47, 48, 49, 112
Elgin, D. S., 88, 90, 144, 173
Ellickson, P. L., 53-54
Endicott, W., 126
Fayol, H., 20
Foley, P. M., 102
Follett, M. P., 71, 75-79, 152
Freeman, R. B., 132
French, W. L., 174
Gulick, L. H., 20
Hackman, J. R., 116-117

Hersey, P., 27, 144, 145
Hogan, J. M., 23
Ivancevich, J. M., 28-29, 138
Jaques, E., 106, 135-138, 173
Johnston, D., 54
Kahn, R. L., 20
Kaplan, L. B., 102
Katz, D., 20
Katz, R. L., 26-27, 144, 145
Katzell, R. A., 23, 101
Krone, C., 99
Kurke, L. B., 24, 63
Landau, M., 89-90, 144, 173
Lau, A. W., 24, 37, 144
Law, J. M., 119
Lindblom, C. E., 29, 90
Mars, D., 126
Martin, S., 24, 33, 38, 63, 66-67, 69, 74, 93, 144, 150
McCurdy, H. E., 8, 40, 46
McGregor, D., 39
McWhinney, W., 99
Menchik, M. D., 53-54
Mintzberg, H., 19, 22, 23, 24, 26, 166
Molloy, E. S., 103, 105
Morgan, B. S., 102
Newman, A. R., 24, 37, 144
Olsen, D., 120
Parkinson, C. N., 48-49
Pascal, A. H., 53-54
Perrow, C., 74
Plous, F. F., Jr., 115
Ramos, A. G., 146-147
Rosow, J. M., 101, 108, 115, 117-118, 121
Ryterband, E. C., 145-146, 173

Salzmann, R. R., 19
Sayles, L. R., 22
Selznick, P., 28, 147
Shartle, C. L., 21
Simon, H. A., 28, 90
Shrode, W. A., 92-93, 144
Soyka, D., 114-115
Stout, R., Jr., 89-90, 144, 173
Stryker, P., 25
Szilagyi, A. D., 28-29, 138
Taylor, J. C., 100, 101
Taylor, F. W., 39, 44-46, 77, 98

Thompson, J., 91
Treadwell, D., 8
Trist, E., 98, 99, 105, 106
Vann, D. H., 23
Wallace, A. M., 113
Wallace, M. J., Jr., 28-29, 138
Walton, R. E., 103
Webber, R. A., 18
Wrapp, H. E., 29, 30
Yankelovich, D., 118
Zager, R., 101, 117-118, 121
Zalenznik, A., 18

SUBJECT INDEX

Accountability, 138-143
Applications of self-managing
 approaches, 163-164
Blaming, 139, 140, 141, 142
Bureaucracy, 135, 136
 inevitability, 173
Bureaucratic controls, 47-48
California
 public sentiments in, 126
 see also Superordinate to subordinate ratios
Computers in decision making, 88, 89, 92, 145
Conception/execution dichotomy, 44
 origins and nature, 44-47
Conceptual skills, of managers, 27
Control versus cooperation, 74-75, 79,
 see also Cooperation versus managing, 89
Cooperation, 71-72, 76-77
Coordination, 20, 72, 76-77, 79
Cutbacks in government 13, 14, 126-127
Decisions, 28-30
 characterizations, 91-92, 94-95
 nonroutine, 28-29, 143-145
 reactive, 92-93
 routine, 28-29, 82-83, 143-144
 see also Discretion
Declining resources, 13, 14, 126
Delegation, 78
Development activities, 34-37, 41, 95, 96
 preferences for, 37-39
Discretion
 constraints on, 84-85
 in decision making, 88-94, 143-144
 at direct service level, 82-83
 factors influencing, 88-92
 in formulating goals, 93-94
 of managers, 143-144
 at middle and upper levels, 83-87

Empirical (school), 22-24,
 see also Private sector, public sector
Employee ownership of firms, 115-116
Error
 prevention, 139, 142
 protection against, 89-90
 tracing, 140,141
Executive abilities, 73
Expectations
 of managers (moderating), 90-91
 of the workforce (changing), 100-102
Experiments in work redesign
 in private sector, 111-116
 in public sector, 118-122
Flexible work schedules, 117-118
Government
 attitudes toward, 125-126
 costs, 13, 14, 169, 170, 171
Grade escalation, 51-55
 City of Los Angeles, 53-54
 DOD, 51-53
 federal government, 53
 Los Angeles Police Department, 54
Hierarchy, 14, 136-137
Human relations, 45, 145-147
 skills, 26-27
Implementation of self-managing
 approaches
 facilitating, 168, 175-176
 obstacles, 167-168
 problems, 164-165, 173-176
 see also Self-management
Labor unions, new role, 115
Local government trends, 126
Management, as a process, 99
 participative, 11, 14, 15, 97, 107, 173, 174
Managers
 decisions of, 28-30
 definition, 18, 43

functions, 19-24
importance, 9, 10, 11, 131, 165, 166
influence, on subordinates'
performance, 64
need for, 165-166
nontraditional, 97-99
preferences of, 37-39
role, 19-24
traditional, 19-32
traits and skills, 25-27
see also Discretion, Expectations
Maintenance activities, 34-37, 41, 95, 96
Myth of management
beneficiaries, 131-132
definition, 129
nature and durability, 129-130
themes counteracting, 143-151
Nonmanagers
ambivalence toward supervision, 65-68, 70
performance without supervision, 62, 64-65
Organizations
and individuals, 74
complexity, size, and information overload, 88
ownership by employees, 115-116
Parks and recreation, example, 153-160
reorganization, 158-160
structure, 154-157
Participation in management, see Management
POSDCORB, 20, 23, 31
Powerlessness, of middle levels, 83-84
Private sector
empirical studies in, 22-23, 25
see also experiments in Work redesign
Professional-technical occupations
growth, 50
Promotion, 136, 137
Promotional opportunities
dearth, 132-133
dilemma, 132-133
Propositions, central, 128
review, 127-128
Public assistance
agency example, 160-163
reorganization, 162
structure, 160-162

Public sector
empirical studies in, 23-24, 34-38, 62-70, 92-94
see also experiments in work redesign
Public and private sectors
differences, 167
similarities, 21, 39-40, 46, 75, 167
Quality circles, 11, 14, 174, 175
Quality of working life, 102-104
Salaries
as factor in redesign, 168-171
savings from, 15, 169
Scientific management, 45-46
challenge of technology, 97-99
Self-management, 15, 104-105, 108, 109, 123, 124, 148, 149, 152, 175,
see also implementation of self-managing approaches
Span of control, 55-59
County of Los Angeles, 55-56
State of California, 58-59
Stratification, 49, 135-137
Superordinate to subordinate ratios
County of Los Angeles, 55-56
Los Angeles Police Department, 54
State of California, 58-59
Superordinate to subordinate
relationship, 14, 18, 19, 150-151
as affected by low discretion of superordinate, 85-86
Supervision
attitudes toward, 11, 12, 66-69
changes in, 64
definition, 62
importance, 10, 11, 61, 62
need for, 12, 13, 64-65, 69, 165-166
and performance, 62-65
see also Nonmanagers
Supervisors
attitudes toward, 11, 12, 66-69
contacts with subordinates, 62-63
Technical skills, of managers, 26, 27
Time-span analysis, 135-137
Traditionalists, in management field, 17-29
versus Mary Parker Follett, 78-79
Traditional strategies
versus new work arrangements, 130-131

Upward grade float, 53-54
Work in America report, 97, 106-109
Work groups
 terms for, 104-105
 autonomous, negative assessment, 106
Work redesign, 97, 111, 123, 124
 critical view, 116-117
 positive assessment, 106-109
 recent trends, 114-116
Workers, nontraditional roles, 97-99
World of Work Report, 112-115, 119-121

ABOUT THE AUTHOR

SHAN MARTIN is currently an organizational consultant working primarily in the Los Angeles area with state, municipal, and county governments, and is also Lecturer at California State University at Dominguez Hills. She received her Ph.D. from the University of Southern California, where she taught in the Applied Behavioral Sciences of the School of Public Administration. Dr. Martin received the Henry S. Reining, Jr., Award in 1981 for her doctoral work. Her interest in bureaucracies, particularly their management and the quality of work life they offer to public employees, extends beyond the United States. She served as consultant to a department in the Civil Service Bureau in Bahrain for one year in 1979-1980, and has written about management training in the Middle East and about the growth of Western-style bureaucracies in developing nations. She visited Brazil in 1982 to learn about efforts to debureaucratize government services, and is currently working on a project to study and evaluate the "Programa Nacional de Desburocratizacaõ" in collaboration with Brazilian scholars and administrators.